Teaching of History

Published by
Lotus Press Publishers & Distributors

Teaching of History

S.K. Sharma

Lotus PRESS

4735/22, Prakash Deep Building,
Ansari Road, Daryaganj,
New Delhi - 110002

Lotus Press : Publishers & Distributors
Unit No. 220, 2nd Floor, 4735/22, Prakash Deep Building,
Ansari Road, Daryaganj, New Delhi - 110002
Ph:.: 32903912 , 23280047 , 09811838000
E.mail : lotus_press@sify.com
Visit us at : www.lotuspress.co.in

Teaching of History

ISBN: 81-8382-172-3

Published by : **Lotus Press Publishers & Distributors**, New Delhi-110002
Printed At : **Afcon Enterprises**, New Delhi

PREFACE

"Teaching of History" is a complete text-cum-reference book for teachers, teacher-trainers and teacher-trainees of all pedagogical institutes and departments of History of different universities.

The present book is designed to highlight the aims and objectives of teaching history; curriculum in history; methods of teaching; dramatization and excussion audio-visual aids; text book and supplementary material, lesson plans has been given in a very impressive manner. This book can prove an effective guide to teachers and teacher-trainees for understanding the psychology of students and their problem and show the right path in the field of teaching.

This book deals with the topics of Teaching of History—Aims, Objectives; Curriculum in History; History Teacher and Environment; Methods of Teaching History; Teaching of Dramatization and Excursion; Audio-Visual Aids; History Textbook and Supplementary Material; Lesson Plans in History; Presentation of History at Different Stages.

All the fundamentals of Teaching has been given in this book which have been drawn from authoritative sources. Yet the simple interpretation makes it an ideal text-cum-reference book.

Publisher

Other Books on

TEXT BOOKS

CONTENTS

1

Teaching of History—Aims, Objectives

The word 'History' has been decided from the Greek word 'Historia', which means *"what has actually happened in the past"*. In fact, history is very precious subject. It tells us about the human civilization of the past days. A famous historian has remarked, "What men have done and said and above all what they have tbought—that is history". In the words of Henry Johnson, "History has always been what human beings thought about the past and an this sense it has always been of creation of the past".

Since Napoleon remarked that 'history is a fable agreed upon', people started thinking that history was not a very dependable thing. In fact, it is not so. Spencer has remarked, "Read them (the act of history) if you like for amusement, but do not flatter yourself. They are instructions".

Some thinkers are of the view that "God monifested himself in history".

Jones says that "History is a precious store-house of the experiences of human race. History is recorded so that people may take advantages of the experiences of the people of the past generations."

In the words of Jones, "History is a veritable mine of life experiences, and the youth of today studies history so that he may profit by the experiences of his race."

In fact, history is a pivot round which other subjects revolve.

Whatever the notions may be, history is an important and interesting subject of study. The students must be encouraged to study this subject. This will help them to derive advantages out of the experience of the past generations. Since the historical and economical interpretations of history has taken an important all the more important subject to study.

Words of Henry Johnson are worth recording in this context: "History is itself a phase of development and therefore, never entirely new. History began as enquiry and is still enquiry. History began as a record and is still a rècord. History became what actually happened, and is what actually happened."

History has been defined in various ways. Some people think that it is a collection of the events only. 'These events are caused by certain factors. It is the history that presents an answer to the causes.

Henry Johnson is of the opinion that history is a detailed account of the events that have taken place. It is evident from definition that history mainly deals with the events of the past. In history there is the description of the events only.

Dr. Radhakrishnan has defined history as "The memory of a nation or a race."

Various educationists and scholars have defined history in various ways. Some think that it is a 'new date calendar', while others have termed it a collection of events of war'.

The best defination, which is scientific to a very great extent, has been given by Rapson. He says:

"History is connectced account of the course of events and the progress of ideas."

This definition lays stree on the scientific organisation of the events.

Old Concept of History

From the above discussion, it is clear that in the olden days and upto the mediaeval times, history deals with the kings and queens, their ministers and courtiers, their generals and warriors, and sometimes national heroes. History was generally written to eulogise royal personalities; the life of the general people was simply ignored. In the olden days, there was no distinction between history and mythology. the main purpose of writing history was *(a)* to eulogise the kings and their warriors; *(b)* to inspire the youth of the nations; and *(c)* to provide entertainment to the people. With all these aims in view, virtues and vices were exaggerated to the great extent. Heroes were made supermen and the oppoenents demons. The original stories had some historical truth in spite of the exaggeration, but they gathered moss in the process of transmission and the process of transmission and the process continued for centuries. Sometimes, the history also served the purpose of religious propaganda. It was the reason that most of the scholars and great men condemned history with the close of the middle ages. Scholars like Spencer consider the historical records as mere stories fit for amusement with no instructional value in them.

Change ia Concept

In the 19th century with the advance of physical sciences attitude of the students of history was entirely changed. Up till now the main aim of study of history was to eulogise the exaggarated past but now its purpose was to understand the actual present with the help of the history of the past. The students of history became very critical and tried to draw the true picture of the past which is the basis of our complicated present. Many learned men collected, criticised and judged the old documents and every effort was made to lift the truth from them.

Concept of Indian History

History in India has an oral tradition. The 'bards' and other people used to learn by heart various events and deeds of the people.

Before the art of writing had developed, there was no writen record of history in India. The historical events were used for literary, artistic, political and religious purposes.

Before the 19th century history was more individual and personal in nature. People did not not believe in presenting an analysis of the society of social actions.

In 'Puranas' and other historical writings of India, events have not been arranged in a systematic and chronological order. There is more of praiseful description of the actions of Kings and warriors by their dependants.

History as a Science

Some scholar are of the opinion that history is a science while others are of the view that it is not a science at all. It is an art only. Before we enter into the discussion, whether history is a sciene or an art, we should have an idea of the science.

Science has been defined as a *'systematic study of knowledge'* concerning the relationship between cause and effect of a particular phenomenon. In order to collect the scientific data and systematised material, science employs various methods.

Strictly speaking. history cannot be termed as a science. Scholars are of the opinion that history is not based upon certain theories and ideals. The facts of history are too complicated and unique. They seldom repeat in the real sense of the word. Historical data are not available for observation and experimentation. Historical facts are the product of human thoughts and actions. Human behaviour is based on free will of the individuals. Therefore human activities cannot provide dependable data for the formulation of general laws. The underlying factors of historical facts are so varied and have such a wide schope that they can seldom be uniform.

Cause of eventes in history is very much influenced by the will power of the individuals. It is not posible for events to move in their own way against will and wish of the people. There is no scope for experiments in history. Like Physical science, there is do set theory or principle on the basis of which the events of history may be put to test.

Sciences are of two kinds, Physical science and Social Science. History is not a Physical Science, but it is certainly a Social Science. It may not employ the methods that are employed in the experiments of Physical Science, but it does employ the methods of Social Science in tbe following forms:

(a) In history we have a collection of the data. These data may be secured from any quarter. The entire data that form history are collected at a place.

(b) The collected data are very cautiously analysed, classified and sorted. The laboratory of history is these, the ingredients of which are obtained by various human beings made of flesh and bones. History may not be a science in the restricted sense but broadly speaking, it is a Social Science.

(c) In the end, after proper observation, analysis and comparative inspection certain principles and theories are laid down. These theories are not like the theories of the Physical Science.

Since history is a Social Science which deals with human life and human actions, we cannot expect the rigidity of the Physical Science from it.

History as an Art

Some scholars are of the opinion that history is an art. Art is nothing but the practical application of the knowledge acquired by science. Art is also a part of literature and fine art. Here we have a display of emotions and find feelings. This element is also available in history. He was on account of this that some scholars went to the extent of saying that history is a part of literature.

History is an art as well as a science. The aforesaid criticism brings us to conclusion that in the history, we have blending of both art and science. When it discovers truth. it is a science and when it establishes and describes those truths, it becomes an art. Thus history is that source in which knowledge and action both go together. Lord Acton has rightly said that the study of history is critical, objective and new. In his statement, he has put in the clements of science as well as art.

CHARACTERISTICS OF THE STUDY OF HISTORY

1. Multisided. As all aspects of the life of a social groups are closely interrelated these happenings should cover aspects of the life of the social group and need not ordinary give predominance to any one aspect of life (*e.g.*, political aspect, which had so long dominated history).

2. Objective Record of Happenings. It is a study of the past happenings in the life of a social group, based on objective evidence as far as possible. Every precaution should be taken to base the data on original sources and make them free from subjective interpretation. The happenings should not be placed before the readers without some indication of the amount of faith which may be placed on their authenticity.

3. Not only Narration But Analysis. The selected happenings should not merely be narrated; the causal relationships between them should be properly unearthed. The tracing of these relationships should lead to the development of general laws which should be able to reveal the real nature of the happenings. Comparison and contrast with the casual relationships existing among similar happenings in other social groups may also be made to improve the reliability and validity of these laws.

4. A Study of the Present in the Light of the Past. The present social life of man in different parts of the world, has evolved through centuries of human efforts in various directions. Modern history enables us to understand how society has come to its present form so that one may intelligently interpret. The matrix of social forces and movements, in the midst of which we are living. It helps us to discover and explain how this adjustment has take place in the past and how it is taking place today.

5. Relevant. Only those happenings should be included in the study of history which are relevant to the understanding of its present life. The present has evolved out of the past and the business of history is to study this evolution. An understanding of this principle should enable one to know which of the past happenings are important for history and which are not.

6. A Scientific Study and a Faithful Record of Our Past. According to its modern concept, history is not confined to one period or country or nation. It starts from the appearance of man on this earth and deals with all places where man has gone and lived. It deals with all aspects of human life—political, social, economic, religious, literary, aesthetic and physical. It is a study of man's evolution on earth.

7. Evolution Growth and Development of Human Civilization. History is not static. It is dynamic growth, development and evolution. "It traces the fascinating story of how man has developed through the ages, how man has studied to use and control his environment and how the present institutions have grown out of the past. Man's struggle with his environment—yesterday and today, man's use and abuse of his powers and resources, his development and the essential unity of human civilization are the main themes of history." Pt. Jawahar Lal Nehru said "Man's growth from barbarism to civilization, is the main theme of history." Great religious and political leaders, philosophers, educators, explorers and scientists, born in different parts of the world, have contributed to the evolution and progress of modern civilization.

SCOPE OF HISTORY

By the term scope, we mean the breadth, comprehensiveness, variety and extent of learning experiences, provided by the study of a particular subject. A brief account of the development of history as a branch of knowledge, reveals the immensity of its growth in depth and extent. What was once only limited to a local saga, became the universal history of mankind, depicting man's achievements in every field of life. There was a time when history was considered a mrere collection of legendary stories, heroic ballads and folk talks, meant to be recited for their moral value and at the same time, to delight the audience. Today no phase of human activity falls outside the field and jurisdiction of history. The subject of history includes not only a study of political activities of man but also a study of his achievements in the physical, social, economic, religious, philosophical, literary, artistic, cultural, industrial, technological and scientific fields, right from the beginning of human life on this earth upto the present day. Thus its scope has become as wide as the world and as long as the existence of man on this earth.

Today we hear of "History of Art," "History of Culture," "History of Civilization," "History of Religion," "History of Music," "History of Geography," "History of Physics," "History of Philosophy," "History of Education," "History of Biology," "History of the Atom," "History of Literature," "History of Mathematics," and History of what not. A learned speaker on a political religious, literary or any other platform connected with any field of human activity, will place before his audience pure simple history, connected with the life and achievements of some past or great human beings and nothing else. Thus the scope of history is almost limitless. It knows no ends. This is clear from the following chart:

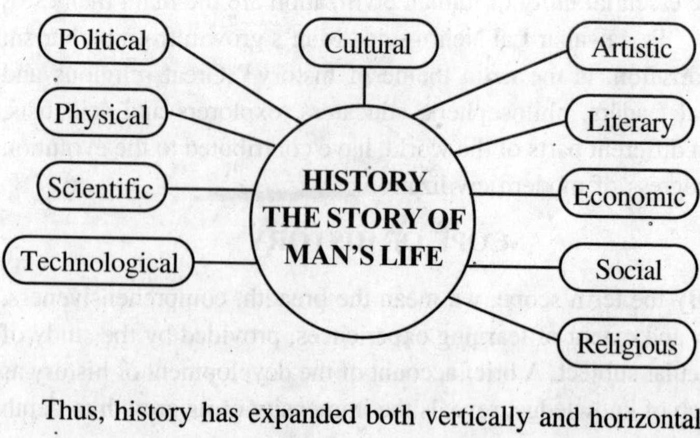

Thus, history has expanded both vertically and horizontally.

HISTORY OF HISTORY

1. **In the Middle Ages.** History was handmaid of theology. The historians were primarily interested in discovering and explaining the Divine Plan in history.

2. **In the 17th Century.** Two major influence *i.e.,* a system study based on the examination of historical authorities and the use of non-literary sources like coins, inscriptions, etc., led to the development of critical history.

3. **In the 19th Century.** By the impact of scientific principles and methods the historians were attracted by the prestige of the physical sciences and they wanted to raise history to the level of a science by applying scientific procedures.

4. **In the Twenteith Century.** There was shifting of emphasis from the political to the economic and social aspects. Marx made an important contribution in this respect. History began to be studied from cultural, economic and social aspects alongwith political aspects. The history became broad-based.

SCOPE OF HISTORY

While defining history, we have seen that it is one of the oldest subjects of study. It has grown with human race, developed with human race, and shall probably end with human race. In other words, it can said that history and man are "inter linked. It is not possible to separate the two. In short, history is a story of the human race from the beginning up to the present day. It deals with various aspects of the development of the human race. In this way, its scope is very wide and varied. It deals with the aspects of human society. Various social religious, economical and political aspects of buman society dealt within history. It studies the progress of the human race in all these aspects.

History does not confine itself to the study of the human race of the present-day or past-days. It studies the past activites of the human race as well. It is through history only that we are acquainted with the past experiences of'the human race. In the light of past experiences, it is possible for mankind to make progress and go ahead. In this way, the history links the present of the mankind with that of the past.

We cannot say that future is outside the scope of history. Experiences of history shall be the experience or tomorrow, and so history is connected with the future as well.

History is connected as already stated with the various facts of the human life. It deals with the intellectual progress of the human race as well. When it describe the activities of great man, it takes a step to influeuce the intellectual progress of human race. It also includes the achievements and deeds of great patriots and warriors. Thus it inspires human race for future as well. In the words of Lord Action, "If the 'past has been an obstacle and a burden, knowledge of the past is the safest and surest demancipation."

E. Lewis Hasluck correctly says:

"A knowledge of history interprets and illumines the whole of human life. It adds to our knowledge of the existing state of world a knowledge in which the human society and institutions have grown up, a knowledge for future."

Bases for Including History in the Curriculum

There is always some reason or the other, which impels educationists to give place to subject in the curriculum some scholars remark that history can neither solve the problem of our bread and butter, nor can it be useful to us in our day-to-day practical life and so it should not find a place in the curriculum. This concept may be correct to some extent, but history does solve our intellectual, moral and spiritual needs. The feelings of justice, patriotism, generosity, sympathy, kindness, liberty, humanity etc., are generated by the study of history. History acquaints us with the qualities of the lives of great men, who existed in the past and who laid their lives in the defence of justice and truth.

Miss Drummond has rightly remarked : "In actual practice too, I have always found that it is a Frederich the Great, Richelieu, or a Walpole, who thought far from moral, has a greater faseination and interest for children, that say, Shafts bury or Florence Niahtingale. The good people are often dull and neither teacher nor taught wants to linger over them."

Therefore, history has a great importance for human race, which at least acquaints the future citizen with the economic, social, religious and political conditions of the past that brought about the proress of the human race. With the help of this knowledge lt is possible for us to make progress in the present and future.

Far Indian student the history has a great role to play:

(a) It teaches Indian ways of life and its development.

(b) Scientific study of history remove the social barriers.

(c) It gives an incentive to the students to develop themselves and make new discoveries.

(d) It improves the mental horizon of a student and he holds the world as his family.

The following extract very clearly lays down the importance of the teaching of history:

"The study of history besides widening to mental horizon of children gives a useful intellectual training. It involves the exercise of memory for assimilating the facts taught and the use of imagination for the past. Science and events which have to be visualised the use of judgement and reasoning and facts and events have to be weighed, conclusions have to be drawn and comparison and contacts have to be made."

The study of history enables tbe childern to asses whether their motherland is progressing on right social, cultural and intellectual Jines. Human culture is known by the students through the study of history. Therefore. the study of history may not have a direct importance in earning bread and butter, but it does have an indirect importance for the lives of young citizens.

We have tried to assess the importance of history. With this importance in view, now let us try to sudy the aims of the teaching of history.

AIMS OF TEACHING HISTORY

Every subject has certain aim with which it is studied. These aims are in consonance with the aims and objectives of the society. For a democratic country, the education should serve the following aims and objectives:

(a) Development of the qualities of ideal citizenship.

(b) Development of qualities of leadership.

(c) All-round development of the personality.

(d) Development of the economic efficiency and character building.

It is not possible to achieve all these aims without studying history. Teaching of history is helpful in the achievement of some of these aims like development of the qualities of citizenship, qualities of leadership character building etc.

Changing Aims

Aims of teaching of history have changed from time to time. In the past the aims to the teaching of history were different from that of today. Previously, history was taught keeping the following aims in view—*(a)* to foster patriotism; *(b)* to develop the trails of heroism in the young warriors and princes; *(c)* to develop communal fanaticism; *(d)* to train the faculties of memory, imagination and reasoning; and *(e)* to give training in politics and to create love for the present type of government. But now, the aims of teaching of history are totally changed. We will discuss here the aims of teaching history in different times.

(i) Aims to teaching of history in olden days. In olden days, history was only a chronology of events. It was intended at preserving the memorable events of life. In those days, history was a part of literature. Then the teaching of history aimed at preserving and keeping in memory the events that had some importance for the people at large. By and by the aims changed.

(ii) Aims of teaching history in the 19th century. Nineteenth century saw the development of of scientific outlook in the various aspects of life. In education also, this attitude found its place. Teaching of history was now based on scientific outlook. It intended that reviving the past events of the society with a view to help the present day set-up.

With the development of the democracy and nationalism, teaching of history assumed a different outlook. It is now considered to be an intergral part of education. Carl Augusts and Muller made a good deal of efforts in this direction. These eductionists thought that history should help the understanding of other subjects of studies. They have laid down the following as the aims of teaching of history:

(a) Understanding the present in a better manner, with the help of the study of the past;

(b) Bringing about the intellectual development of the children, and

(c) Helping the study and understanding of other subjects.

(iii) Aims of Teaching History Today. Today, we see that there are definite aims laid down for the teaching of history. These aims are based on scientific outlook. Various thinkers and scholars have tried to assess and study aims of teaching of history. These aims are enumerated below in brief.

Aims according to Miss Drummond

Miss Durmmond has written a book *history in schools*. In this book, she has tried to make a thorough study of the aims and objectives of the study of history. She has tried to lay down the following aims for the study of history.

(a) Interest for the study of history—The first aim of the teaching of history is to create interest in the future. Thus history has also to be stabilished. History, in fact, is a treasure of knowledge so its study can be very useful for young children.

John Dewy, the fumous American educationist, has said that history is to be studied not because it is an account of the past but because it helps us to understand the present. Similarly Morley has remarked that: "It is the present which really interest us, it is present we seek to understand and explain. I want to know what man thought and did in the 18th century, not out of diletante or idle antiquorian curiosity but because the 18th century was at the root of thought and action in the 19th century."

It is possible to stabilise interest of the students in the study of history when the teacher is capable of linking the past with the day-to-day life of the present.

(b) Formation of a Scientific Outlook. The study of history should aim at the development of the scientific outlook in the students. Their power of imagination should be developed with the data provided by the history.

(c) Developments of International Outlook and Understanding. Today, we are living in an era of international understanding and outlook. We cannot live unless we are able and prepared to understand the outlook of the people of other countries. Study of history would enable the students to develop this outlook.

According of Prof. Linwood chase, the aims of teaching history should be as follows:

(1) The method of collecting the data pertaining to history.

(2) Evaluating the contributions of the past.

(3) To develop the consciouness in the educants about society and social values.

(4) To help the students to have correct ideas about the importance and meaning of liberty and freedom.

(5) To help the students to understand the influences of historical facts and situations upon life.

(6) To develop the spirit of patriotism.

(7) To help the students to understand the series of social changes and their importance in social progress by linking the past with the present.

(8) To inculcate interst in the study of history and to encourage them to have a proper idea of the time place and their relationship.

(9) To understand the sequence of historical events from the time immemorial.

(10) They have an idea of the historical facts and to give them a practical shape so as to have their utility in life.

(11) To study the development of human race according to time.

Aims of Teaching History According to American Commission on Study in History

This Commission was appointed by the College of Entrance Examination Board. On the basis of the enquiry, it has laid down the following aims of the teaching of history :

(1) To give an idea to the student that the society is ever progressing.

(2) To develop the sense of social responsibility in the students.

(3) To acquaint the students With those problems and difficulties that faced the human race in the past and in the present times.

(4) To impart the knowledge of history to the students in such a way; that they may know the use of the informations acquired; know that art of examining' the events in an objective manner, may have a scientific study of the data and lay down theories and rules on the basis of the study, obsevation and classification of the data.

Right of History to Get a Place in the Curriculum

It is rather necessary to give place to history in the Curriculum. It is a Social science which broadens the mental horizon of students and helps them to have the social knowlege of progress. There are other reasons as well for it to get a place in the curriculum of the schools.

Values of Teaching History

Teaching of history has certain values as well. Before we talk of the values of teaching history we should have, an idea of the difference between the aims and the values. The aims are nothing but the set objectives according to which the teacher acts. He directs his teaching according to those aims and objective. Values are the gains of those aims. In fact of achieve those values when we have acquired to aims. It has rightly been remarked: Aims are an end in itself and values are the product.

According to the Memorandum of Cambridge University, values have been defined in the following words:

"Amidst the multiplicities of values the bewildered teacher may legitimately ask what the procedure should be; whether he should regard history from an intellectual standpoint, *i.e.*, as a training of the intellect or view. It has a literal and broadening influence or from the ethical standpoint has a training hand, right living, and character; or even whether he should concerntrate solely on imparting a body of knowledge, living time, and reflection to the rest."

The teacher of history should be very clear about the values of teaching history. He should try to develop in the students, a series of ideas that would lead to the achievement of those values.

A Few Values of Teaching History

Following are a few values of teaching history:

(1) Through history, an attempt is made to enrich the knowledge of the students on the basis of the past experiences. An attempt is also made to develop the spirit of sympathy and self-confidence.

(2) It leads to the intellectual development of the child. The child tries to employ his intellect in the solution of various problems children, when they study the deeds of great heroes like Rana Pratap, Shivaji or Razia Begum, feel to be like them. If this thinking could be given a practical shape, it shall be very useful for the students and the society at large.

(3) It develops in the students the qualities that may help them to adjust themselves with society.

(4) Teaching of history can generate, in the students the interest of studying the deed of great men. This interest helps them to employ their leisure in the study of the lives of great men and women. With this study, their feelings are directed towards the high ideals and values.

(5) Through the teaching of history, an attempt is made to inspire the students to achieve great deeds.

(6) Teaching of history also strengthens the relationships between the teacher and the taught.

(7) Through the study of history it is possible to develop effectiveness in our life.

(8) Serious students of history can develop the qualities of partiotism, ideal citizenship and service for the motherland. It is possible for the students to develop all these qualities when the teacher has given a real turn to their interest and talents.

(9) It develops the power of reasoning and thinking in the students.

(10) It also develops in the students, the quality of objectivity and impartiality. It encourages them to take up the service of makind without any self-interest.

Teaching of History with National Outlook

The political and social unity is the demand of the day in India. The study of history is not essential for social integretion. It teaches the students:

(i) To honour the contribution made by various sections and minorities.

(ii) To understand the unity in Indian culture.

(iii) To make the students understand their past and to prepare them to know that they are the rightful claimants of unified culture; and

(iv) To make the students understand that whatever progress the country has made, is due to co-operation and friendly relations in various sections and communities in India.

(v) To let the students understand the interdependence of various atmospheres.

OBJECTIVES OF TEACHING OF HISTORY AT VARIOUS STAGES OF EDUCATION

Objectives at the Primary Stage

The following objectives should be kept in mind while teaching history to the children of the primary schools:

(1) To Develop in the Students the Interest for History. In or to develop the interest, the students should not be burdened witht the information and the fear of examination.

(2) Development of the Power of Imagination. The power of imagination is an essential characteristic of childhood. Through the teaching of history, an attempt should be made to awaken the power of imagination of the students. This can be achieved by teaching history through story-telling method. Children are very fond of stories and so it is natural for them to get interested in history if it is taught through story-telling method.

(3) The Students have to be Made Concious of the Fact that their Present Life is very much influenced by the Past. Sense of time should also be developed in the students. It can be done with the help of time charts, time curves, time graphs etc.

(4) Spirit of Patriotism and World-brotherhood should be Developed in the Students. At attempt should be made to inculcate the spirit of patriotism and world-brotherhood in the students.

Objectives at the Junior High School Level

Teaching of history to the students of the Junior High School level should be done with the following objectives in mind:

1. The real interest in the history should be developed in the students.
2. Various mental faculties of the children should be developed. They should be encouraged to take up independent thinking.

   Critical faculty should be developed in them. They should be encouraged to look at various historical facts from a critical point of view.
3. The sense of time, as developed at the primary stage, should be further developed. More abstract means should be employed to develop this sense of time.

4. Patriotism and world-brotherhood should be developed in greater respect.

5. The students should be encouraged to look at the present in the light of the past, and also to dream future.

Objectives at the Higher Secondary Level

At the Higher Secondary level, teaching of history should be carried on with the following objective in view.

1. Interest in the study of history, as developed at the primary and junior stages, should be strengthened and consolidated.

2. Their sense of time, as developed at the primary and junior stages of education, should be strengthened and consolidated. A scientific outlook should be developed in them.

3. Mental faculties of the students should be so developed that they may acquire the power of reasoing and arriving at the decisions. The students should be encouraged to examine things critically and accept them only when their power of reasoning accepts them.

4. They should be acquained with the 'Law of Cause and Effect.'

5. The students should be given ideas of the exchange of the various cultures of the world. They should be made to realise that every country of the world has to depend upon the other with regard to its culture in one way or the other.

6. The students should be encouraged to judge the present in the light of the past. They should also be made capable of looking forward.

7. They should also be tuaght about the development of the civilization of the world.

8. The students should be acquainted with the social political and religious problems of the society. They should also be acquainted to be able to solve those problems.

Conclusions

1. Teaching of history is important from various considerations. It acquaints the young souls with their past.
2. The history must find a place in the curriculum.
3. Teaching of history should aim at the development of the qualities of ideal citizenship, leadership, economic efficiency and character.
4. It should bring about an all-round development of the personality of the student.
5. In olden days, the teaching of history was different from that of the modern days
6. In a democratic and nationalistic set-up, the teaching of history is done with different aims.
7. Miss Drummond has laid down the following aims of its study:
   (a) Interest in the study of history.
   (b) Formation of scientific outlook.
   (c) Development of international outlook & understanding.
8. At the primary stage of education, teaching of history is intended to inculcate in the students *(a)* the interest for the study of history; *(b)* to enable them to understand that the present is influenced by the past; and *(c)* to develop in them, the feeling of patriotism and world-brotherhood.
9. Prof. Linwood Chase and American Commission on the Study of History have laid down certain aims of the

teaching of history. All these aims are intended to acquaint the students about the past and to enable them to have an idea of the present in the light of the past.

10. There are ethical, cultural, social, disciplinary, informative and nationalistic values of teaching of history.

8. Teaching of history is also done with *(a)* utilitarian aim, *(b)* intellectual aim, as well as *(c)* social, *(d)* national, and *(e)* moral aims.

9. Objectives of teaching of history are different at different stages of education.

OBJECTIVES OF HISTORY AS SUGGESTED IN 'GUIDELINES AND SYLLABI FOR UPPER PRIMARY STAGE' (NCERT, 1988)

A. Objectives of History at the Upper Primary Stage (Class VI to VIII)

1. to develop an understanding and appreciation of the dynamics of the ethic diversity of India;
2. to promote an understanding of the major stages in the evolution of Indian society through the ages;
3. to develop an appreciation of the growth of various components of Indian culture in different parts of the country in different periods;
4. to develop an appreciation of India's cultural heritage and its composite nature, of its richness and variety, and of the processes through which it has developed.
5. to develop a critical appreciation of the past so that the pupil's personality is free from irrational prejudices and bigotry, parochialism and communalism, and is imbued with a scientific and forward-looking outlook;

6. to develop the ability to study contemporary problems of Indian society in their historical perspective;
7. to develop an understanding of the process of change so that an appreciation of the aspiration for change to establish a just social order is inculcated;
8. to deepen knowledge about the understanding of India's freedom struggle and of the values and ideas that it represented;
9. to develop an awareness of the necessity of an participation in the work of preservation of historical remains.
10. to promote the study of the historical devleopment of India in relation to and in the perspective of the history of mankind as a whole.

B. Objectives of Teaching History at the Secondary Stage (Class VI to X)

The general objectives of teaching history from Class VI to X, as a part of general education, may be as follows:

1. to develop an understanding of the evolution of human societies and civilizations in general and of Indian society and civilization in particular;
2. to develop an understanding of the processes through which human societies have changed and evolved;
3. to inculcate an appreciation of the contribution of different peoples to the progress of mankind as a whole;
4. to develop an understanding of the integrated nature of historical development and of the homogeneity of civilization;
5. to develop an appreciation of the growth of various components of Indian culture and legitimate pride in the achievements of the Indian people in different periods and in different parts of the country;

6. to develop an integrated view of Indian history and civilization and of human civilization as a whole;
7. to help develop a spirit of enquire and the ability to think critically and creatively and to differentiate between the obsolescent and the dying and the living and the emerging;
8. to develop an historical perspective for understanding contemporary India and the contemporary world of current problems and contemporary processes of change; and
9. to develop critical appreciation of the past so that the pupil's personality is free from parochialism, irrational prejudices, bigotry, communalism and every kind of chauvinism and is imbued with a rational, scientific and forward-looking outlook.

C. Objectives of Teaching History in Classes IX and X

NCERT (1988) has suggested the following objectives to teaching history in classes IX and X.

1. to promote an understanding of the process of change and development through which human societies have evolved;
2. to promote an understanding of the foundations of human civilization and appreciation of the basic unity of mankind;
3. to foster the understanding that the mutal interaction of various cultures has been a major factor in human progress;
4. to develop an appreciation of the contributions mad by various cultures to the total heritage of mankind.
5. to enrich the understanding of those aspects of Indian historical development which are crucial to an understanding of contemporary India;
6. to facilitate the study of the history of specific countries and regions in the general perspec time of world history at a later stage;

7. to develop a world historical perspective necessary for the understanding of the contemporary world.

Instructional Objectives of School Subjects (1989) has listed the following instructional objectives of history at the Secondary Stage.

1. Knowledge Objective
2. Critical and Logical Thinking Objective
3. Understanding Objective
4. Practical Skills Objective
5. Interests Objective
6. Healthy and Social Attitude Objective

These objectives have been further explained as under:

1. To acquire the knowledge of terms, concepts, facts, events, symbols, ideas, problems, trends, personalities, chronologies, generalizations, etc., related to the study of History.
2. To develop the understanding of terms, facts, principles, events, trends, etc. related to the study of History.
3. To develop the ability of critical and logical thinking.
4. To develop practical skills helpful in the study and understanding of historical phenomena.
5. To develop interests in the study of History.
6. To develop healthy social attitudes.

Objectives and Their Specifications

1. To Acquire the Knowledge of Terms, Concepts, Facts, Problems, Trends, Events, Ideas, Personalities, Chronologies, Generalizations, etc. Related to the Study of History.

Specification of the Objective

To demonstrate the achievement of the above objective, the pupil:

(i) recalls facts, terms, concepts, events, etc.

(ii) recognises facts, terms, concepts, events, etc.

(iii) reads information presented in various forms.

(iv) shows information on maps, charts, diagrams, etc.

2. To Develop and Understanding of Terms, Facts, Principles, Events, Trends, etc. Related to the Study of History.

Specifications of the Objectives

To demonstrate the achievement of the above objectives, the pupil:

(i) classifies facts, terms, concepts, etc.

(ii) compares and contrasts the events, trends, concepts, etc.

(iii) identifies relationship between causes and effects, means and ends, etc.

(iv) arranges facts, trends, etc. in a particular known order.

(v) discriminates between the significant and insignificant, important and less important causes, events, etc.

(vi) illustrates events, trends, etc. by citing examples.

(vii) summarises.

(viii) interprets the maps, charts, extracts etc. from the different source of the History.

(ix) detects errors in the statements and rectifies them.

3. To Develop the Ability of Critical and Logical Thinking.

Specifications of the Objectives

To demonstrate the achievement of the above objectives, the pupil:

(i) identifies the problems.

(ii) analyses the problems.

(iii) interprets problems with implications.

(iv) verifies the inferences.

(v) selects relevant facts, principles, etc.

(vi) sets up hypothesis.

(vii) advances arguments in support of contentions.

(viii) draws inferences and generalizations.

(ix) establishes relationships.

(x) predicts.

(xi) evaluates.

4. To Develop Practical Skills Helpful in the Study and Understanding of Historical Phenomena.

Specifications of the Objectives

To demonstrate the achievement of the above objectives, the pupil:

(i) draws historical maps, charts, diagrams, etc.

(ii) prepares models, time freezes, etc.

5. To Develop Interest in the Study of History.

Specifications of the Objectives

To demonstrate the achievement of the above objectives, the pupil:

(i) collects coins and other types of historical material.

(ii) prepares illustrative materials, aids, etc.

(iii) visits places of historical interest, archaeological sites, museums and archives.

(iv) reads historical documents, maps and charts.

(v) participates in historical dramas and mock presentations of historical events.

(vi) plays an active role in the activities of the History Association.

(vii) writes articles on historical and other related topics.

6. To Develop Healthy Social Attitudes.

Specifications of the Objectives

To demonstrate the achievement of the above objectives, the pupil:

(i) establishes friendship with pupils of other communities and faiths.

(ii) acquires and displays a sense of patriotism.

(iii) shows repsect towards other people's opinions, ideas, beliefs, and ways of life.

(iv) reads about other faiths and religions.

(v) practises the spirit of noble ideals.

(vi) co-operates with others in social and civic activities.

(vii) appreciates cultural variations.

(viii) appreciates and supports the need for settling disputes among nations in a peaceful manner through world organisations like U.N.O.

(ix) believes in the equality of man irrespective of caste, creed, religion and colour.

(x) appreciates the contributions made by various civilizations.

(xi) appreciates the interdependence of nations and peoples.

VALUES OF TEACHING HISTORY

The analysis of the aims and objectives of teaching history makes it evidently clear that the value of its study is cultural, humanising and disciplinary. The liberalising effect of the study of history flows mainly into three channels. It enables the pupils to develop an understanding of the cultural heritage; it provides them with intellectual training and it inculcates in them moral virtues. Its worth as a means of rousing patriotic fervour, as a vast store of knowledge and as a source of satisfying pupil's sense of interest cannot be minimised.

1. Cultural Value. Man is the heir to all ages. One of the main motives of history teaching has been to convey to the pupils the rich heritage of the mankind. The study of history develps an understanding of the different forces which have shaped the destiny of man and paved the way for his development in society. The knowledge and understanding of these forces and the appreciation of the heritage, bequeathed to us by the past generations equips to work for the further enrichment of this culture.

(i) ***National Needs.*** How much and in what from the cultural heritage of mankind is to be conveyed to the child is decided according to the needs of the society. The demands of a nation are not to be ignored particularly in India where fissiparous tendencies and forces of disintegration are playing havoc with our national sentiment, where communalism, casteism, regionalism and linguism are raising their hydra-head again and again. Hence appreciation of national heritage is necessary.

(ii) ***World Culture.*** As we are the members of the world society. Sutdy of the ways of life of the people of different countries down the ages would inculcate the feeling of universal brotherhood and foster philanthropic attitude essential for creasting world understanding.

2. The Ethical Value. History teaching initiates the pupils in the ways of great men and women wholed noble lives and made valuable sacrifics for the cause of humanity. It develops in them a sense of appreciation for the selfless services rendered by them for the benefit of mankind. Boling-broke says, "History is philosophy teaching by examples how to conduct ourselves in all the situations of private and public life." In the same vein Froude declares, "History is a voice for ever sounding across the centuries the moral laws of right and wrong."

Limits of Idealisations. The idealisation of the so called greatmen—the national heroes-has resulted in the distortion of the facts of history. Their good qualities have been overdone and bad qualities of their adversaries highly exaggerated. The criterion of their greatness or otherwise has been their success and failures. But as Miss Drummond point out, "...It is easy to see the wicked flourishing in the past as well as in the present, and in the history lesson the wicked have to be dealt with as well as the good.... The good people are so often dull that neither teacher nor taught wants to linger over them." The same warning is issued by Jarvis. When he says, "We must beware of teaching that goodness always prevails, that wickedness must ultimately receive its deserts. To do this is to lead the children to measure goodness by success and to train them to love justice and goodness and truth not for themselves alone, but for the sake of the materials benefits which are supposed to acurue.

It is not the exclusive domain of history to provide moral training through the study of great men of the past ages. Joffrey says, "If all the history books were burnt, we should not be destitute of exemplary material for use in moral education; we should still have the greatmen and women of our own days, and also the resources of imaginative literature."

So far as the behaviour of man is the theme of history, so long as history is concerned with man as an individual and as a member of society, great men will be studied. The need is to make a judicious slection and an objective presentation of the facts.

3. Educational Value. The imagination of the children is developed through the teaching of history. When a teacher narrates a stody, the pupils try to form mental pictures of the scenes described. But the formation of correct pictures of images in the mind of the children depends on how the story is introduced. The teacher's duty is to relate the story in clear and unequivocal terms. If he wants to infuse some idea. Thus he will help the children to visualise the relice of the past ages, and to take a keen interest in them. Jarvis says, "If we invest with the charm of romance, old ruins, old manuscripts, old remains of any kind, that are reminiscent of other times, our pupils will learn to regard them with reverence, demanded by their age alone, even part from association."

4. Intellectual Value. A large number of intellectual values are supposed to accrue from the teaching of history, It sharpens memory develops the power of reasoning, judgement, imagination and memory. It cultivates the qualities of reading, analysis, criticising, and arriving at conclusions. This generalisation is based on the basic assumption of faculty psychology which considered mind as an aggregate of several independent and isolated powers and certain subjects were considered suitable means to develop these faculties.

Other teachers contended that with the biological conception of mind as an organic entity, theory of faculty psychology does not hold good. It is not the exclusive domain of history to provide mental training but other subjects also provide intellectual discipline. We cannot introduce history in the school curriculum only on these grounds.

History is the record of the past actions of man with its manifold and myriadic appeals. It touches nearly all the aspects of life. It is a vast storehouse of knowledge where pupils can search at will. "It can satisfy in a unique way", as C.P. Hill suggests, "the growing child's curiousity about other people, about their lives, personalities, deeds and ideas; and it can awaken an imaginative wonder and excitement about the whole world of humanity, past and present.

5. Nationalistic Value. Many teachers think that history teaching instils in the heart of the pupils a sense of patriotism. It provides them with the knowledge of the affairs of their country which is essentail to make them worthy citizens. The children should be made aware of the problems that the country had to face. They should be filled with patriotic fervour to work assiduously for the good of their country. However this 'partiotic fervour' should not pass into 'my country right or wrong' attitude. World had to pay a very heavy price in terms of a large scale distruction of human lives and human culture in the wake of two world wars which were the outcome of blind glorification of the past and chauvinistic ideas accruing from them. Teachers should provide unbiased study of the national history in the wider perspective of the history of the world.

6. Internationalistic Value. The domain of history is very extensive and wide. It tells the tale of many societies. It broadens our mental horizon, makes us cosmopolitan in outlook and imparts catholicity of vision. The study of widely different and diametrically opposed group of human beings with their divergent customs, traditions, laws and at various stages of development, makes us believe that behind this outward diversity, there is cultural affinity between man and at a higher plane of human existence, these differences sink into an all-embracing unity as all are advancing towards the same goal. The realisation of this essential unity of human race is the first step towards fostering universal understanding based on the virtues of tolerance, kindliness, love, sympath and goodwill.

IMPORTANCE OF LOCAL HISTORY

The well-known maxim 'Proceed from known to the unknown' and proceed from the 'concrete to the abstract' and the guiding stars in the teaching of history. Hence, there is a great importance of teaching of Local history. Local history not only covers the historical events of the place, village, city or town and district where the student resides but it also covers the history of other neighbouring places and that of the environment. It is not only limited to the historical study of the town or village there the child lives. It includes the history of the neighbourhood. There are old ruins, castles, buildings of historical values, temples and other historical relics around every locality. Visits to such sites are very fruitful in the study of the subject.

Now the concept of history is totally changed. It is not only the story of kinds and queens. Its main aim is to help the children in reading their present through the study of the past. This aim can be achieved only by giving importance to the teaching of Local history. The children should realise that what they are studying in the subject of history, will actually influence their lives, and they will thus take keen interest in the subject.

Local surveys give valuable training in history. The children know their customs and traditions and their outlook is broadened. The students take keen interest in the Local history because it is concerned with their ancestors. By the teaching of Local history, the students can be trained to have emotional feeling towards their region and work for its development. Local history develops amongst the students the scientific outlook and they believe a thing right or wrong only when they see it from their naked eyes. Local surveys give valuable training in history. These are as useful as laboratory work in the teaching of science. The children should be ennourged to make their note-book of Local history and record the history of the village or the town in which they live, the history of some important families and the history of some historical sites around them. Such training will serve as a basis of advanced historical studies. E.L. Hasluck has penned down the importance of Local history in the following words—"The study of Local history is a real importance and should most certainly find some space, however small, in the shcool history syllabus. It helps and brings home to the pupil, by everyday contact with historical scenes, names and buildings, the sense of the development which his country has undergone, and removes his thoughts from time to time away from the present to the contemplation of the ages that are passed.

Teaching of Local History of Different Stages of Study

It is true that the Local history is of great importance, but the teacher should not wholly depend upon the Local history. It should serve just to illustrate and illuminate National or International history. It should be taken as supplementary study. Local History is of great importance to the students of primary classes as well as to the students of junior classes. It teaches the boys to respect the customs and traditions of that place because they are germs of the life of the citizens. Due emphasis should be given to the Local history at the primary and higher secondary stages. However, in the higher classes, Local history is no so much important. It must be taught but it shall not be of great use for the students of these classes. At the higher secondary stage, the students should be asked to take excursion to the neighbouring places. They should be encouraged to collect materials from the different parts of the locality which are of historical buildings of their locality and their impact upon the social life. They should be encouraged to collect models, specis, coins etc., and take pictures of the different material of historical importance.

Method of the Study of Local History

While teaching Local history, the following methods may be employed:

1. Excursion and tours should be arranged for the places that have importance in the Local history.
2. An attempt should be made a present a history of the local community and social groups.
3. Students should be encouraged to have a look at various places of historical importance in the locality.
4. They should be encouraged to have knowledge of the history of the names of the roads of the locality.
5. An attempt should also be made to present before the students, a history of the various changes that have taken place in the locality, in political, social and economic life.

6. During the teaching of history at the higher classes, the teacher should often refer to Local history to illustrate how past is still influencing us and how we are the product of the past.

From the above, it is clear that the Local history will be of great use if it is taught in the right manner. However, it should be kept in mind that the feeling of regionalism may not develp among the students by the teaching of Local history. Local history should serve the purpose of developing the nationalism amongst the students. They should be encouraged to consider the things in the right perspective and develop scientific outlook.

KINDS OF HISTORY

History is the story of the progress of mankind since times immemorial. In fact, if we take history from this point of view, we shall come to the conclusion that there is one history of the whole world. Since man came into this world, he has been making progress continually. This *story of progress is history*. This story stretches even to the farthest corner of the world. Historians, for the convenience of the study, have divided this story into various parts and types. Every part is complete in itself. No one can be called a historical if he has read only a part of this long and varied story.

Bases of Classification

While dividing the story of progress of mankind, historians have kept in view the geographical boundaries. The history of the world has been split up in two parts—*(a)* National history, and *(b)* Regional history. These two histories have further been split up and classified into various categories along with the classification of the history on the basis of place or geographical area.

The Basis of the Classification of the History is the Time or Period. It is on the basis of this that history is called as Ancient History or Modern history.

The Basis of Classification is the Circumstances or Conditions. According to religious, social, political and economic circumstances, history has been divided into various types. On the basis of this, we come across Political history, Economic history, Social history and Religious history.

Types or Kinds of History

On the basis of the discussion given above, we shall try to present the following classifications of kinds of history:

(1) Classification of History on the Basis of Space or Geographical Boundaries *i.e.*, Concentric Method. On the basis of geographical boundaries or space, the history may be classified under the following heads: *(a)* History of World, *(b)* History of the Nation, *(c)* History of the Region, and *(d)* Local History.

All these histories put together, shall present a composite picture of the events of the entire world. We shall now try to talk about them a bit in detail.

(a) ***History of the World.*** In regard to the teaching of history of the world, there are two schools of Thought. One is of the opinion that it should not be taught to the children at the lower stages of education. This is meant only for the students of higher classes.

On the other hand, the second School of Thought says that the students must be given a glimpse of the World history. This shall not be difficult for them. On the other hand, they shall evidence curiosity in it. They shall also acquire acquaintances with the ways of living of the people of the other countries. This is based on the Child psychology. These thinkers go to the extent of saying that while presenting a picture of the history of the world to the children, an attempt should be made to start this at the earliest possible ages. Such a presentation shall awaken greater curiosity in the students.

Both these Schools of Thought have their own arguments. Now educationists have come to realise that at the secondary level of education, the history should be taught in the background of the World history. This background may be sketchy only. It should not deal with the details of the World History.

Educationist agree that early history of the world must be introduced in the syllabus at a early stage to form a background. After this the teacher should freely make references to the World history while teaching national or local history. The preliminary course of the World history should also be very short and simple. We may have a short course of World history again at the end of higher secondary stage.

(b) ***Local History.*** Local history is the history which deals with the local environment of the child where he resides. it is not merely the history of the village, city or town where the student resides but it also deals with the local environment and the events of neighbouring places. The teaching of local history is very important. We have dealt with the importance of the local history in Chapter V of this book.

(b) ***History of the Nation or National History.*** The world has been dividend into various geographical boundaries known as countries or nations. Every nation has a history of its own. History of the nation should be presented before the students in a collective manner. Although every state has different traditions and conditions within its geographical boundary, yet an effort should made to present the history as a single unit. History of India is a clear example of this thing. Here we have a variety and diversity of traditions of Gujarat. These states have the history of their own. The teacher of history should try to present a comparative

picture of these various histories of various units, but while doing so, he should not let the unity or the spirit of oneness slip of his hands.

(d) ***History of the Region.*** Every state has been divided into various regious and states. There are similar units in every country Historians have divided history into various regions. Such a classification may be useful from the point of view of study, but in the present age of internationalism, it may prove harmful. It leads to narrowing down the outlook. An attempt should be made to teach the students the Regional history in such a way that it does not develop regionalism and provincialism in them.

(2) Classification of the History on the Basis of the Time, *i.e.*, Chronological or Periodical Method. An attempt has been made to classify the history on the basis of time. From this point of view, the history has been classified into following categories: *(a)* History of the early ages, *(b)* Ancient history, *(c)* Mediaeval history, and *(d)* Modern history.

(a) ***History of the Early Ages.*** This history delas with the times when people lived in Stone age. That was the time when man had started living on the earth. The life in those days, was very difficult. It was difficult to get food, clothes and places of dwelling. Man had to take to hunting, to the trees for covering his body from the open sky or the shade of the tree was his adode. Story of these early ages are of great iterest to the children. Children should be acquainted with these circumstances so that they may have a knowledge of the development of the civilisations and the struggle that the man had to face in his early years.

(b) ***History of the Ancient Ages.*** After stone age, man made some progress. This led to the development of the society. He started doing certain religious and social acts. Society, according of functions, classified itself in various categories.

Some art and literature also developed. Heroes and warriors continued to dominate the scene. By this time, social consciousness had developed a lot. This period deals with the history of this age.

(c) ***History of the Middle Age or Medieval Ages.*** During this period, human civilisation progressed a good deal. From the Indian point of view, this is called the period of Rajputs and Muslims. So far as the religious conditions are concerned, it was the age of multifarious religious. It will not be wrong to call it a period of religious and political activities.

(d) ***Modern Period.*** Modern period is the period of the highest development of culture and civilisation. Various political Social, economic and religious changes have taken place during this period. Science, literature, art, etc., have worked woders. It shall not be wrong to call it an Age of science. It is an Age of Space Conquest. Man has established his supremacy not only over the nature but over the space as well. Every day the train of progress is going ahead. Modern history deals with all these things.

(3) Classification of History According to the Conditions and Circumstances, *i.e.*, Typical Method Things. According to the circumstanes and conditions, history has been divided into the following types: *(a)* Political history, *(b)* Economic history, *(c)* Religious history, and *(d)* Social history.

(a) ***Political History.*** In regard to the classification of Political history, scholars have different opinions. Some scholars are of the view that all the aspects of the Political history should be studied properly. This no only satisfies the human curiosity but also enables the students to have a knowledge of the political events of the past. Along with the political development, social traditions and cultural events are also to be studied.

On the other hand, some scholars are of the opinion that Political history should not be sudied in a narrow manner. In other words, it means that the deeds of the rulers and the Political changes should not be the sole concern of the study. Along with the political events, other factors should also be kept in mind.

(b) ***Economic History.*** Since Karl Marx, Economic history has achieved a significant place. Karl Marx has very clearly laid down that it is the economic condition that determines and influences the progress of the society and the human beings. Political events are guided by the requirements of the economics. State, society, culture, literature, etc., all are dependent upon economic circumstances. In short, Karl Marx has given the central place of Economic history. From this point of view, the study of Economic history is very important.

While studying Economic history, an attempt should be made to assess other types of events as well. It should not be studied in an isolated form. This history is not very useful for the students of lower classes. In fact, it shall be beyond their comprehension. It should be studied at the higher secondary stage and after that.

(c) ***Religious History.*** There is a class of educationists that lays great stress on the study of Religious history. It says that religion has influenced our civilisation and culture since the early ages. All the political and social events have taken place only on account of religion. From this point of view, the study of Religious History is very important.

While studying Religious history, we should keep in mind that we do not look at religion from an universal and human point of view. It should be treated as a collection of virtures and good qualities that are helpful for the preservation of human race.

While teaching Religious History, the teacher has to be very cautious. He has to present things in a very objective manner. He should not criticise any religion because this is likely to hurt the susceptibilities of the followers of that religions.

(d) ***Social History.*** This branch of history deals with the development of the family and its problems, social institutions, their organisations, traditions, education, agriculture, literature, etc. In facts, its material is very broad and vast. Social events are also linked with political events and so, indirectly social history deals with political history. The teacher of the Social history should try to deal with the subject in an isolated manner.

□

2

Curriculum in History

History curriculum is the part of the school curriculum primarily intended to promote self-understanding. It gives proper conception of time, space and society. It enables the pupils to evaluate the achievements and values of their own age. It teaches tolerance. It cultivates valuable intellectual attitudes. It broadens the intellect. It teaches moral principles. It cultivates a forward look. It imparts mental training. It helps in resolving contemporary social and individual problems.

As an independent subject or a part of environmental studies or social sciences history forms an important part of the high school curriculum. It is included as a separate subject in classes XI and XII. It is usually an optional subject. The primary purpose of its inclusion is to widen the horizons of the students. All parochialism is undesirable. For a proper understanding of one's immediate present it is very necessary to understand and appreciate it in its wider context of space and time. In terms of space, it implies seeing one's immediate spatial environment in the context of the wider world. In terms of time it implies seeing the present age among other ages. The present cannot be understood in isolation of past. History is a continuous process.

The study of history shows that the world of man is not stationary. It is subject to constant and continuous movement, change and development. History helps in understanding contemporary processes of change, of movement. as well as of continuity.

It makes us aware of the variety and diversity in humanity as well as of unity which makes for a more or less balanced personality. It promotes independence of judgement and an attitude of appreciation of contemporary processes of change. It depends the child's awareness and understanding of the society in which he lives from his immediate environment to the country and to the world as a whole.

PRINCIPLES FOR SELECTING HISTORY CURRICULUM

1. Principle of Functional Relationship. The history curriculum in each class should be well connected with the previous and the succeeding classes.

2. Principle of 2 A's. Age and ability of the students. Personalities, events and ideas in history should be taken up at the primary, middle and secondary classes respectively.

3. Principle of Comprehensiveness. The history curriculum should enable the students to comprehend the present world of human activity and thought.

4. Principle of Emotional Integration and National Unity. Content of the history curriculum should lay emphasis on inculcating values of emotional integration and national unity.

5. Principle of Correlation. Effort should be made to correlate historical events with cultural, economic, political and social events.

6. Principle of Objectivity. No effort should be spared to present material free from prejudices.

7. Principle of Integration with the Daily Lives of the Common Man. History has four dimensions; people, places, time and ideas. All these are indispensable for making the story of humanity intelligible. Today the focus of history curriculum has changed from the life and work of heroes, kings and queens and important personalities to the evolution and growth of societies in all their aspects.

8. Principle of International Understanding and Peace. History curriculum should stress the importance of inter-communication and cooperation among different nations.

Drawbacks of the History Curriculum in India

K.P. Chaudhary points out the following drawbacks in the history syllabi in our country:

1. Lack of Uniformity. There is no uniformity among the different states in regard to the class in which history study may be first introduced. There are states in which the study of history is begun as early as class I while there are others where it is begun as late as Class VI.

2. Neglect of Regional and World History. The syllabuses in all the states over-emphasise national history (*i.e.*, Indian history) at the cost of world and regional histories; nearly 93 per cent of the time available for teaching hisotry (taking all the school classes together) in almost all the states was devoted to the study of Indian history alone.

3. Confused Meaning. Again history is presented to the pupils in the first year under different names in different states; some of the names used are 'History and Civics', 'History and Geography', 'General knowledge'. This means the syllabus framers had no clear conception of what is exactly meant by the term history.

4. Page Limits. There is a belief, among the syllabus framers, that the history syllabus may be made easier by limiting the number of pages of textbook to be written; so, in certain states the number of pages of the textbook was indicated in the syllabus. Because of the anxiety of the textbook writers to include all the facts relevant to a topic and to make their treatment synoptic in order to keep the size of the book within the number of prescribed pages. This makes the history textbook of lower classes more difficult.

5. Poor Gradation. The history syllabus of most states, suffers from poor gradation of the subject-matter included in it. Almost the same facts in Indian history have been presented from class to class.

6. Study of Great Britain. Even in 1954, there were quite a few states, which provided for detailed study of the history of Great Britain, which could not be justified by any of the aims of the study of history which have been accepted.

7. Cultural Epoch Theory. Certain states are still following the Cultural Epoch Theory in framing the history syllabi, though the theory had been rejected long ago. Difficult and abstract concepts have been introduced as early as in classes I and II because according to the Cultural Epoch Theory the ancient period of history is considered to be easier.

8. No Single Consistent Approach. Usually three kinds of approaches are followed in presenting historical facts. In the order of difficulty value they are the story, the biographical and the historical approaches. But in the history syllabi framed for different classes in different states no single approach is consistently followed. For example, in a syllabus for class VIII there are topics like Babar (biographical approch) and the Mughal Civilisation (historical approach). This creates confusion in the minds of the pupils, teachers and textbook writers with regard to the nature of history and the purpose of its study.

9. Lack of Link. Some topics in the syllabuses are isolated (political and military) episodes without any central link between them.

THE NCERT (1976) CURRICULUM APPROACH

Primary Stage. 'The Curriculum for Ten Years' states, "The primary concern of the school at this stage should be to develop the necessary social skills values and attitudes that would enable the child to contribute his mite, as he grows, towards the development of the society to which he belongs."

"During the five of primary school the child's mental horizon would be gradually widened from the home, the school and the local community to the world. In the process, the child would begin to appreciate the geographical elements of his environment. Various human activities, which help him to understand how the gifts of nature are processed to produce goods for serving the various needs of man, would also be studied. He would also get an ideas of the social and cultural life in different parts of the country as well as of some different ways of living in certain parts of the world. Stories and narratives about personages and events that have contributed to our national heritage and human heritage will also be studied. In addition to these, the child would get ample opportunities to develop socially desirable habits, attitudes and values besides becoming broadly acquianted with the functioning of political and social institutions."

Middle Stage. History at the middle stage should acquaint the pupils with the growth of Indian society from prehistoric times to the present. It is necessary to change the emphasis from dynastic history and political details to social and economic conditions and the growth of various aspects of culture in different parts of the country. At the same time a broad perspective of the history of mankind as a whole should also be provided.

The organisation of the syllabus and the selection of the content may be based on the 'patch' approach. In the light of the requirements of general education it is not necessary to give a continuos chronological account of the history of India in the sense that every decade or century of Indian history is covered. Representative periods or 'patches' in chronological order, dealt with in all their important aspects may be given. This may be combined with the 'topical' approach in that in a parrticular 'patch', a few aspects would be selected to be studied in greater detail than other aspects.

The class-wise distribution of the Indian history syllabus may be as follows: Class VI-Ancient India; Class VII-Medieval India; Class VIII-Modern India. With each of the these major periods of Indian history, a broad perspective of the contemporary history of makind as a whole should be provided.

Class IX and X. A systematic course in the history of mankind from prehistoric times to the present day should be introduced for classes IX and X. This does not mean a chronologically continuous narrative but the selection of 'patches' that have a certain unity and distinctiveness along with many diversities. The main basis of selection of these patches may be the successive stages of distinct social formations that existed in different parts of the world in specific chronological periods. The main focus of this course should be on the study of social systems in their rise and growth and their replacement by new forms, and on scientific and cultural development. The historical development of all the major areas of the world, including pre-colonial Africa and the Americas, should be covered. The selection of the content should be based on the specific histories of individual countries only where these histories have a significant bearing on the general history of mankind and represent new trends which became relevant to the history of mankind as a whole.

THE ISHWAR BHAI PATEL COMMITTEE (1977) ENVIRONMENTAL STUDIES

1. Environmental Studies, Class I and II

1. *Our school :* teachers, building learning.
2. *Our family :* life, structure and functions.
3. *Our home :* shelter, facilities, love.
4. *Our neighbourhood :* life, work cleanliness, space.
5. *Our earth :* features, vegetation, water, minerals.
6. *Our sky :* lights, heat, weather, stars.
7. *Man's life :* interesting imaginative stories.

2. Environmental Studies (Social Studies), Class III

1. *The world we live in :* Continents, oceans, our country in the world.
2. *Life in our country :* food, clothing, occupation, language, festivals.
3. *Life in the district :* setting occupation, festivals.

4. *Life in our state :* Location, relief, vegetation, resources, occupation, communications.

5. *Institutions which help us :* panchayat, cooperatives, health centres, education, transport.

6. *Our heritage :* stories of great men and women and of early man.

3. Environmental Studies (Social Studies), Class IV

1. *India :* physical divisions : mountains, plan, rivers and plateaus.

2. *India :* resources : human and national (soil, water, minerals).

3. *India :* transport and communications: on land, water and air, post and telegraph and telephone.

4. *Indian heritage I:* monuments, music, dances, religions, scripts, languages, handicrafts, festivals.

5. *The people of India :* National symbols and festivals, one country.

6. *Indian heritage II :* Stories of famous rulers, reforms, writers scientists, saints.

7. *Our freedom struggle :* Briefly through some of the more prominent leaders.

4. Environmental Studies (Social Studies), Class V

1. *The globe and map of the world :* Hemispheres, equator, poles, tropics, arctic circles.

2. *India and neighbouring countries :* many ways of living; life and occupations in some distinctive areas of the world, *e.g.,* Tundra, Savannah, Desert, Equatorial, Mediterranean.

3. *How we govern ourselves :* the state and central governments, fundamental right, directive principles, duties of a citizen.

4. *Our shrinking world :* transport and communications, land, sea, air, radio, television, newspapers, cinema, satellites.

5. *The changing world :* stories of scripts, numbers, trade, money, discoveries and scientists, Columbus, Galileo, Newton, Einstein. Great men: Socrates, Lincoln. Lenin, Tolstoy, Mahatma Gandhi.

6. *The United Nations :* cooperation among nations, work of UNICEF, WHO, UNESCO, India in the UN.

HISTORY CURRICULUM

1. Class VI, Ancient India

1. Prehistory; Man as a nomad; discovery and use of metals; Invention of the wheel farming.

2. The Harappan Culture; Cities; Occupations; Religion; Script.

3. Life in the Vedic age; Settlements; Economic and political life-Religion.

4. The Mauryan Empire; Persain and Greek invasions; Chandragupta Maurva; Asoka; administration.

5. Rise of Magadha; Kingdoms and republic, emergence of towns: Jainism and Buddhism.

6. India from 200 B.C. to A.D. 300; Satavahanas; Cholas, Pandyas; Cheras; Shakas, Khushanas.

7. India from A.D. 500 to A.D. 800; Harsha; The Deccan and South India; Art and architecture.

8. The Age of the Guptas; Administration: Trade; Religion; Art; Science.

9. India and the World; Rise of Islam; The Arabs in India; India's contacts with other countries.

2. Class VII, Medieval India

1. India from A.D. 800 to A.D. 1200; Kingdoms of South; Religion; Architecture; The struggle for Kanauj; Turkish invasions; Religion; Art and architecture.

2. The Sultanate of Delhi; Mamluks; Khaljis; Tughlaqs; the Bhamani and Vijayanagar kingdoms; Sufi and Bhakti movements.

3. The Advent of the Mughals and the Europeans; Kingdoms in the Deccan; Renaissance in Europe; Voyages of discovery.

4. The Mughal Empire; Akbar; Jahangir and Shahjahan: Aurangzeb; Rise of the Marathas; Art; Architecture; Literature.

5. Decline of the Mughal Empire; Invasions; Rise of independent states.

3. Class VIII. Modern India

1. India in the Eighteenth Century; Expansion of the Maratha power; Society and Polity.

2. The rise and growth of British empire in India; The Carnatic wars; The British conquest of Bengal; British paramountcy.

3. Administrative structure of the British empire in India; Civil-Judicial revenue system.

4. Impact of British rule on Indian economy and society up to 1975. The village economy; Industry and Trade; Educational and Social reform.

5. The Revolt of 1957; Causes; Nature; Results.

6. Reorganisation of the British empire in India; The Act of 1858; Civil Services; Policy of Divide and Rule.

7. Rise of Indian Nationalism and the Struggle for Freedom; The Indian National Congress; Partition of Bengal; the

Gandhian era; Civil Disobedience; The INA; Quit India Movement.

8. Changes in Economy and society after 1858; Agriculture and Railways; Plantations; Industries; Economic conditions; Social Life; Education; Social and Religious Reform movements; cultural awakening.

9. Achievement of Independence; Immediate problems.

4. History of Mankind (Class IX and X)

1. Prehistory; Stages of evolution and development; Palaeolihic and neolihic.

2. First Civilizations (Bronze Age); Egypt; Mesopotamia, India China.

3. Ancient Civilizations (Iron Age); Contribution and influence of ancient Greece, Rome, India and China, Rise of world religions.

4. The Medieval Europe and Asia; Developments in Europe; West Asia; India and China, Feudalism.

5. Capitalism; Industrial revolution.

6. Revolutionary and Nationalist Movements; American War of Indepndence; Nationalist and Democratic Movements.

7. The Renaissance and Rise of Nation States; Rise of towns and cities; Learning, discoveries and exploration; Scientific development; Nation States; Colonization.

8. Imperialism (up to 1914); Important causes and results.

9. The Socialist Movement; Growth of socialist ideas and movements; Russian Revolution.

10. World after World War II; United Nations, Cold War; Technological development.

11. Emergence of Asia, Africa, Latin America, Importance of the Third World; Developing countries.

12. The world from the World War I to the end of World War II; Causes, events and results of the World War I; Fascism and Nazism; Causes, events and results of World War II.

13. The contemporary world and India; International peace and cooperation; New economic order.

HISTORY SYLLABUS BY NCERT

As suggested by NCERT (1988) the classwise organisation of the syllabus may be as follows:

Class VI	:	History
Class VII	:	Medievral India
Class VIII	:	Modern India

Class VI: Ancient India

Unit I	Introduction A. How and why we study the past B. Geographical and Ethnographical, Features of India (Pre-Historic culture of India)
Unit II	The Harappan Culture
Unit III	New Cultural Pattern in India (150 B.C. to 600 B.C.
Unit IV	India from the Rise of Magadha to the Mauryan empire
Unit V	India during the period 200 B.C. To 300 A.D.
Unit VI	India from 300 A.D. to 800 A.D.

Class VII: Medieval India

Unit I	India and the world
Unit II	India from 800 A.D. to 1200 A.D.
Unit III	India from early Thirteenth to early Sixteenth Century

Unit IV	Advent of the Mughals and the Europeans
Unit V	India under the Mughals
Unit VI	Disintegration of the Mughal Empire

Class VIII: Modern India

Unit I	India and the Modern World
Unit II	The Rise, Growth and Impact of British rule in India
Unit III	Revolts against British Rule
Unit IV	British policies and Administration in India after 1858
Unit V	Changes in Economy and Society
Unit VI	Rise of Indian Nationalism and struggle for freedom.

Curriculum Prescribed by Central Board of Secondary Education Delhi

HISTORY

CLASS IX

One paper of 3 hours

SYLLABUS AND UNITWISE WEIGHTAGE

Units

1. Pre-History (Introduction)
2. Bronze Age Civilization
3. Early Iron Age Societies
4. Early African and American Cultures and Civilizations
5. Beginning of Modern Age
6. The Medieval World
7. Capitalism and Industrial Revolution
8. Revolutionary and Nationalist Movements

CLASS X

One paper of 3 hours

THE CONTEMPORARY WORLD HISTORY

Units

1. Imperialism
2. The First World
3. The Russian Revolution
4. The World from 1919 to Second World War
5. The World after the Second World War
6. Cultural Hritage of India
7. Indian Awakening
8. India's Struggle for Freedom

CLASS XI

ANCIENT INDIA

Unit I	Introduction Importance of Ancient Indian History The Stone Age The Chalcolithic Cultures The Harappan Culture
Unit II	New Cultural Patterns in India (1500 B.C.—600 B.C.)
Unit III	The age of the Buddha (600 B.C.—325 B.C.) Jainism and Buddhism. Emergence of Territorial States and the Rise of Magadha State and Society in the Age of the Buddha
Unit IV	Age of the Mauryas
Unit V	Successors of the Mauryas (184 B.C.—A.D. 300) Western and Central Asian Contacts and their Results Early States in South India The Age of the Satavahanas Trade and Towns in Post-Maurya Times

Unit VI Age of the Guptas and after. Rise and Growth of the Gupta Empire. Urbanisation and State froms in Eastern India

Unit VII India's Cultural Contacts with Asian Countries. Transformation of the Ancient Phase

MEDIEVAL INDIA

Unit VIII Introduction, medieval period in the World History India from 8th to 12th centures. The Delhi Sultanate (1200-1400)

Government and Economic and Social Life Under the Delhi Sultanate

The Age of Vijayanagar and the Bahmanis (1330-1585), Struggle for Empire in North India (1400-1523),

Cultrual Development in India (13th-15th centuries), Struggle for Empire in North India

Struggle for Empire in North India

Mughals and Afghans (1525-1536)

Consolidation of the Mughal Empire (Age of Akbar)

Decan and South India (upto 1656)

India in the First Half of the Seventeeth Century. Clmax and Disintegration of the. Mughal Empire (1658-1707).

CLASS XII

MODERN INDIA

Unit 1 Introduction: Construction of Modern Indian History

Unit 2 Indian States and Society in the 18th Century

Unit 3 Beginning of European Settlements

Unit 4 British Conquest of India

Unit 5 Structure of Government and Administrative Organisation of the British Empire in India (1757-1857)

Unit 6	Economic, Social and Cutural Policy of the British Empire in India (1757-1857)
Unit 7	Social and Cultural Awakening in the First Half of the 19th Century.
Unit 8	The Revolt of 1857
Unit 9	Administrative Changes after 1858
Unit 10	India and Her Neighbours
Unit 11	Economic Impact of the British Rule
Unit 12	Growth of New India: Nationalist Movement (1858-1906)
Unit 13	Growth of New India: Religious and Social Reforms after 1858
Unit 14	Nationalist Movement (1905-1918)
Unit 15	Struggle for Swaraj

CONTEMPORARY WORLD

Unit 16	Introduction: A Broad Survey of the Historical Background of Contemporary World
Unit 17	The World from about the end of the 19th Century to the end of the First World War
Unit 18	The World from 1919 to 1939
Unit 19	The Second World War
Unit 20	The World after the Second World War
Unit 21	Policy, Economic and Society in the Contemporary World
Unit 22	Development in Science, Technology and Culture
Unit 23	The Future Outlook, Major issues and problems. International cooperation

❑

3

History Teacher and Environment

ESSENTIAL TRAITS OF A HISTORY TEACHER

I. Scholarship. Acquaintance with problems of present-day life; background of a liberal education; reader of magazines and newspapers; reader of books on the subject taught; sound knowledge of the subject taught.

II. Professional Training. Desire for improvement; professional attitude; reader of professional books; reader of educational magazines; sound professional training.

III. Personality. Physical aspects; passive virtues; executive virtues.

(a) **Physical Aspects.** Personal appearance including dress, carriage, social expression, mannerism and personal cleanliness; etiquette including good manners, observance of social forms, courtesy and refinement; voice, rich and mellow; good language command including pronunciation, enunciation and grammar; health.

(b) **Passive Virtues.** Enthusiasm; fairness; friendliness; optimism patience; self-control; sincerity; sympathy; tact; understanding.

(c) **Executive Abilities.** Adaptability; directive ability; industry; initiative; organising ability; resourcefulness; self-confidence, self-reliance.

IV. Human Relations. Relations with students; relations with collegues; relations with parents; relations with school personnel relations with administrators, inspectors, supervisors, etc.; relations with the community; relations with publishers, stationers, sports delaers etc.; relations with professional organisation and workers.

ROLE OF THE HISTORY TEACHER

A history teacher is a successful guide, wide awake, an active, enlightened and well informed person. He must listen to new broadcasts, telecasts, read current events, attend lectures and discussions, study and analyse reports and editorials, participate in school and community relations and see good newsreels and documentaries. R.S. Kimball has observed, "Current affairs can be taught successfully when a teacher is sufficiently interested himself. The varying degrees of success however seem to indicate that the ability of the teacher, rather than the quality of the medium or the method is the determining factor. Almost any device can be used effectively. The teacher's own enthusiasm, her own understanding of what should be accomplished, are the matters which determine the failure in success of current events teaching. The best available media fail in their purpose when used by a class guided by a teacher unskilled in methods of current events instruction."

QUALITIES OF A HISTORY TEACHER

1. Objectivity. The history teacher's job is not to indoctrinate but to equip students to make decisions based on sound and objective knowledge. His objective duty is not to select for the student but to point out to him the choice which he may make himself and a method by which such choices may be made. He is perhaps always the focus of public eye more than others because of the very nature of his subject-matter, dealing it does with the contemporary scene. He must discuss issues that are considered controversial and therefore he must be doubly careful to pursue his investigations and teching with objectivity.

2. Deep Knowledge of the Subject. The primary task of history teacher is to get his students to learn. 'Lack of subject preparation stands near the top of virtually every list of causes of teacher failure.' The teacher, 'must know, broadly and deeply, the field in which he teaches.

3. Well Informed. The contents of modern history changes as rapidly as the world changes. The children of the present generation grow up in a rapidly changing, moving and accelerated universe. They want latest and up-to-date knowledge. Therefore, the teacher of history should be keenly interested in latest developments in economics, social, political and cultural life not only of his own country but also of the world at large. He should also acquire a broad under-standing of the family community, state, nation and the world.

4. Skilled in the Use of Technological Aids. A history teacher is expected to possess adequate skill in the use of various aids which enable him to bring vividness and attractiveness in the lesson. Skill in map drawing is also very essential.

5. A Good Communicator. Only a good communicator can guide a discussion stimulate interest and create in the classroom an environment which is rich in materials and where pupils are challenged to work and learn together. A history teacher, should be a good story teller and man of imagination.

6. Application of Field Study Theory. Teachers of history should early get into the habit of "field study" i.e., an application of a field theory to the process of learning both for themselves and for their students. Each problem that comes up for investigation and learning is a field of inquiry which can be examined from many different points of view and by drawing upon the knowledge of many different disciplines.

7. Widely Travelled. First hand information of the important and significant cultural, geographical and historical buildings and places, art galleries, musems, dams, factories and projects, etc. will greatly help the history teacher to enrich and vitalise the teaching of history. It will also enable him to develop breadth of outlook and width of understanding to interpret the culture of different parts of the country and the world of his pupils and this promote emotional, national and international understanding.

8. An Interpreter of Various Experiences. While discussing the functions of a teacher, M.L. Jacks has observed, "Above all he is an interpreter—interpreting not only the experiences to his pupils but also the community to which they belong its past no less than its present, its purposes and its efforts to achieve those purposes, its cultural and technical achievements, its opportunities and possibilities, the invitation to service which it extends and the rewards, glittering or dimly discovered which it offers." A history teacher is in a very advantages position to bring together the past and the present, the new and the old, the alien and the native, the near and the distant.

Academic freedom does not imply the right of indoctrination. James High of the University of California say, "An opinion, derived by any means, if made the sole content of teaching and set up as the 'right' answer, constitutes indoctrination and cannot be countenanced under the guise of academic freedom." Schools are for the purpose of broadening the horizons of the students. Means employed must be objective and honest differences of opinion accepted. It is the duty of the school system to encourage reflective thought. Continued interest in the preservation of academic freedom throughout all ranks of society must stem originally from the schools. Reflected thought concentrated on the records of the human past result in wisdom of the exerise of human choice in the future. Critical, constructive and tolerant attitude is a great part of adequate citizenship and all efforts have to be made in the teaching of history to realize this objective. A history reacher has to perform this task very intelligently and skifully.

The school is a temple of learning and its devotees i.e., children should be kept away form controversial issues. The conflicts of the real world must not enter into the portals of this temple and conflicting issues must not find their way in it. If they enter, they are likely to vitiate the classroom environment. According to Richard E. Survey basically teaching acts comprise the following:

(1) Clarifying with the children the issue that lies at the heart of the concern.

(2) Guiding them in identifying the different choices possible for deciding the issues.

(3) Guiding them in an analysis of the facts and ideas to determine bases for opinions.

(4) Encouraging them to explore the facts and ideas which support the issues.

(5) Guiding them towards suspended judgement.

The history teacher should encourage the students not only to make their own choice as of the moment, but to think more about it and to be on the alert for more pertinent information. He should feel free to express his own favoured choice for action and to substantiate it but should point out that he too is limited in what he can do about making the final decison. He can somewhat assuage fears by suggesting that the other choices for action have strengths to be considered.

SOME CONTROVERSIAL ISSUES IN HISTORY

A. Indian History

1. Date and Extent of Valley Civilization.
2. Origin of the Aryans.
3. Period of the Vedas.
4. Epic Age
5. Nature of the Invasions of Mahmood Ghaznavi
6. Babar's Religious Policy
7. Akbar as a Great King
8. Religious Policy of Aurangzeb
9. Shavaji and Afzal Khan

10. Aurangzeb's Responsibility for the Decline of the Mughal Empire.
11. Causes of the Failure of the Sikhs as in the Anglo-Sikh Wars
12. Happenings of 1857
13. Impact of Macaulay on the Indians
14. Impact of the British Rule
15. Responsibility for the Partition of India
16. Kashmir Issue
17. Reorganisation of the States
18. India's Foreign Policy
19. Centre-State Relations
20. Ram Janmbhoomi Babri Masjid Controversy
21. Punjab Problem
22. Assam Problem
23. Reservation Policy

B. World History

1. Vietnam Issue

2. Role of the UNO in Promoting International Peace and Cooperation.

3. Ban on Armaments—Nuclear and Coventional

4. Neo-Colonialism—A Threat to International Peace, Security and Co-operation

5. Nambiar Problem

6. Rhodesian Problem

7. White Regime in South Africa: a Menace to Peace

8. Non-Aligned Summit Movement.

9. Socialist and Communist Ideas.

THE HISTORY ROOM, LIBRARY AND MUSEUM

The history teacher of today is becoming more concerned with the facilities required for, doing good work. Different types of aids, text-books, reference books, pamphlets, maps, charts, projectors, models, magazines and pictures etc. are available to his teacher. This material cannot be satisfactorily used without a separate history room. It this room all this material can be stored and the teacher can immediately get it for use as the occasion demands. A history room, with a pleasant social climate, becomes a learning laboratory in which great emphasis is laid on student activity and student participation in class-room procedures. The pupils feel at home and have an incentive to work. "Class-room furnishing and their arrangement have a direct bearing upon the quality of results obtained. Satisfactory outcomes can be expected from any class-room situation, only when adequate and comfortable working facilities are provided." A well-equipped history room is essential for fostering a historical attitude of mind among the pupils.

QUESTIONS AND ASSIGNMENTS

1. What is the place and importance of text-book in the teaching of history ?

2. It is sometimes argude that good teaching is impossible if the pupil confines himself or herself to a single text-book. How far do you agree to this statement and why ?

3. What are the advantages of using a good text-books?

5. Discuss the different types of history text-book ? Which of these types would you recommend for use by your students and why?

6. What are the essential qualities of a good text-book of history.

7. Discuss the good ways of using a text-book effectively.

For utilizing these new approaches like problem Method, the Project Method and the Source Method a special setting and adequate equipment are essential which can be provided only in a separate history room.

Essential Equipment

A little bigger than the usual class-rooms. This history room should be furnished separately to provide for instructional work, demonstration, practical handwork and group work. This requires the following material in history room.

1. Chalk-board. Chalk-boards may be black, green, white, yellow or of any other soft colour. On such boards, chalks of different colours are used for drawing outline pictures as well as for writing summaries and important words, phrases, headings and sentences. Generally located at a place in front of the room which may be comfortably visible to the pupils. The chalk-board to the most important visual aid of the instruction.

2. Furniture. New, light and movable furniture is a source of great convenience to students as well as the teacher. Seating arrangement is of great importance. Flexibility and usefulness are important factors of this arrangement. Single chairs and tables for students are the best. The same purpose is served by a single adjustable desk-chair combination. Seating arrangement will depend upon the type of activity undertaken by the students. Single tables may be joined together in a circular or semicircular shape to form a suitable commitee table for discussion, planning and reading. History class-room should be provided with a movable desk or table and a chair for the teacher. A table dictionary, desk calender, a pad, a pen etc. should be provided for the teacher's use.

3. Bulletin Board. Every history class-room should be provided with a bulletin-board located along one of the sides or at the back of the class-room. It represents a many-purpose teaching aid. It relates to the work in progress. Displays on it include pictures, poster, pamphlets, cartoons, graphs, maps, charts current, news-items, features, articles, paper cuttings, magazine articles and samples of pupils' creative work.

4. Books and Book-cases. Books are essential for a history room as a test tube and other apparatus for chemistry laboratory. Among books there should be text-books by different authors, printed source books, current magazines, periodicals, encyclopaedias and reference books The students should have an easy access to the reading material. Open book-shelves should be provided for this type of material.

5. Museum. Old coins, old clothes, dresses, utencils and historical relics like old paintings, sculptural works, art pictures etc. may be got collected through history students.

6. Flags of Different Nations. Specimens of flags of different nations of the world, with explanatory notes, where essential, should also be kept in the history room. Special reference may be given to the history of our National Flag.

7. Audio-Visual Material. The history class-room should be equipped with a variety of audio-visual material including pictures, maps, charts, graphs, diagrams, posters, cartoons, slides and a fairly large globe. A 16 mm projector and screen, an opaque projector, a record-player, a radio set and a tape recorder may be kept in the history room.

8. Tools and Supplies. Pupils must be furnished with a variety of working material needed by pupils for practical work in history including daints. Water colours, coloured pencils, ink, pen-holders, brushes, rulers, compasses, erasers, scissors, blotters, special papers of different sizes and colour, paste, paper clips, drawing sets, pins, nails and various other things.

9. Cabinets and Files. Cabinets and files are essential in a history room for storing various materials. It is always beneficial to label all folders ; boxes and drawers that contain specific articles. A system of filing the material is very helpful for locating various things. After finishing their work, the pupils should be directed to return all materials to their proper places in the cabinet. Regular supply and consumption of material should be entered in a stock register. One of the pupils should be made responsible for the supplies during the year. The teacher should evaluate the materials occasionally and discard those thing which have no further value in learning.

Class-room Management

Healthy social relationships must develop between pupils and teachers in a history room. In the words of Moffatt and Howell, "Class-room management expresses a business like and orderly approach to the teaching-learn situation. Leadership gives direction and provides for the type atmosphere so essential for effective instruction. Good organisation for all activities eliminates confusion and possible discipline problem pupils should, therefore, be encouraged to develop abilities and attitude commensurate with the democratic sharing of responsibilities in co-management of their own class-room." Each pupil should be given the opportunity to assume some responsibility for a definite period of time. Student committees under student chairman should be formed in the beginning of each academic year for distributing and collecting material, for the arrangement of equipment, for selecting and organising displays on the bulletin board for securing and purchasing books, magazines and other material, for wecoming guests, for contacting outside agencies and establishments, for arranging entertainment, programmes, for organising excursions and educational tours and for assisting the teacher in various ways. They will provide training for group leadership and committee cooperation, so essential in a democratic society. Each student should be encouraged to show his work opportunities for self-discipline and self-control, based on cooperative should be provided to all pupils leading to character building and personal development.

Class-room Laboratory Work

In addition to regular class periods in history some periods may be utilised for laboratory work. The main purpose of laboratory work is to develop skills, original thinking, planning and creative expresses among the pupils. In the laboratory periods the pupils draw maps, prepare graphs, charts, time lines, models or pictures solve problems, work on projects and answer given questions and assignments individually or in groups. Specific directions are given to them about the work to be done and sources from where the material is to be Collected. They try to learn through research and exploration. They are free to move about the class-room and make use of the material, pertaining to the work in hand. Although time is fixed for the completion of each activity or unit, yet they are permitted to progress according to to their own ability and capacity. The teacher acts as a guide and a director. He gives suggestion, guidance and encouragement when the pupils are in difficulty.

HISTORY LIBRARY

History library is an important centre of resources for instructional programme in history. It provides a variety of material for instructional in work, guidance to teachers for curriculum construction and in the selection of good book and help the pupils in reading and to adults in the locality, in counselling and guiding. It lays the foundation for free enquiry and intellectual development.

Library as a Resource Centre

Not merely a depository of books history library a resource centre extensively used by all members. As a resource centre, it reaches every class-room, every pupil and teacher and even the community. It helps the teacher to enrich curriculum and facilitate personal and professional reading. It helps the student to gain meaningful experiences in reading, thinking and forming independent judgments. It provides for recreational and hobby interests to the community. It is also a store-house of all types of teaching aids including maps, charts, pictures, models, manuscripts etc. Which are easily accessible to all concerned.

Functions of the History Library

1. Providing Materials for Instruction and Reading. History library renders valuable service to both the teacher and the pupil by facilitating the instructional programme for the teacher. It provides a lot of reading material to the pupil for answering questions, doing assignments and solving problems independently.

2. Stimulating the Reading. The school library not only makes text and reference books available to teachers and pupils, but it also has a number of books of general interest. Interesting story-books biographies, books on adventure, travel, inventions and discoveries etc., motivate pupils and stimulate reading for enjoyment and recreation. It this way, effective reading skills are developed in the pupils.

3. Providing Opportunities to Pupils to Assume Responsibility. While the pupils are taught how to keep the books with care, they are also provided opportunities to serve on library committees, to act as library assistants and to do other odd jobs connected with library service. Thus, they learn to work in co-operation with others, to help other pupils in the selection of books and to assist them in the solution of some of their problems.

4. Teaching the Techniques of Using the Library. The history library also teaches the techniques of making proper use of the variety of materials, it contains. A definite procedure is followed in purchasing, organising, storing, issuing and receiving books, periodicals, pamphlets and other aids and materials, placed in the library room. Definite rules are observed for getting, keeping and returning books and other materials. Definite hours are fixed for library service. Definite discipline prevails in the library and reading rooms.

Essential Equipment for History Library

1. Shelving. In the library room shelves should be adjustable if valuable space is to be conserved. These will not only contain books of all types but also albums of records, films, filmstrips, school made slides and the like arranged in a definite subject and section wise order.

2. Tables and Chairs. The tables should be of proper height and size and the chairs, strong and comfortable to accommodate students and teachers who are to read and work in the library. The librarian should be provided with a separate chair and desk for facilitating him to discharge his duties most effectively.

3. Racks for Newspaper and Magazines. Daily newspapers as well as history journals and magazines in different languages should be placed in different racks, especially got prepared for this purpose. These racks are to be placed in different corners of the library room or in the reading room, attached to the library so that teachers and pupils may come and read them in their vacant periods.

4. Filling Cabinets for Catalogue Cards. These should be got prepared very carefully so that drawers may he of a standard size to accommodate catalogue cards very easily.

5. Bulletin Boards. These are used for displaying book-jackets and other illustrative material to advertise new arrivals in the library for those who are not regular visitors.

6. Store Room. The store room will store old hooks newspapers the History Room, Library and Museum and magazines as well as equipment, which is essential for audio-visual material.

Important Library Resources for History

1. Book Resources

(1) Text Books. A number of good text-books on various periods of Indian History as also history of the world and history of other important countries, must be made available. Keeping in view the excavations in different parts of India and also in other parts of the world and the of rapidly changing human life in the modern age, new and revised editions of standard text-books should continually be purchased for the library, to supply up-to-date knowledge and information to teachers and students.

(2) Literary Materials. These include biographies, autobiographies, fiction folklore, short-stories, travel books, books of adventure, herostories, romance, drama and poetry.

(3) Reference Materials. These include reference books, encyclopedias, dictionaries, year books, biographies, atlases, biographies, directories, old manuscripts, old coins and other excavated material, Govt. Gazetteers and the like.

(4) Source Materials. These include source books, manuscripts, original accounts of travellers and contemporary historians diaries, proclamations, original letters and despatches of kings, Governors and Viceroys, treaties, old monuments, historical buildings, sites, old tools, weapons, armours, coins and the like.

2. Non-Book Sources

At the field of history is closely connected with current events in the rapidly changing world, books should be supplemented by periodicals, pamphlets, newspapers, journals, magazines and other such materials. These can be very easily and inexpensively utilized for instructional purposes:

(1) Periodicals. Periodicals include not only current events magazines but also those which depict various aspects our of life, including art, literature, music, dance etc. because these depict the social trends of the period.

(2) Pamphlets. Pamphlets of various types are very useful for history teaching. Usually written about one specific topic or aspect and generally illustrated with pictures, photographs and drawings, they are generally very cheap because they are mostly published .by various government agencies and bureaus for specialized services.

(3) Special Documents and Publications etc. These include brochures, yearly calendars or data books of activities within the states published the state governments in India and folders, containing rich information about various places, regions and towns. This is a valuable resource of primary source materials.

(4) Newspapers. Newspapers are published in English and in various modern Indian languages. A local newspaper, is very essential for every library because it highlights local happenings, issues, personalities and developments. One or two other daily newspapers of all Indian circulation in regional and national languages are also desirable for school library. There will enable the students to keep themselves well informed of all that is happening around them in the national and international fields.

(5) Audio-visual or Non-reading Materials. History library should also house large variety of non-reading materials. Among the important visual materials may be included pictures, photographs, illustrations, maps, charts, cartoons posters, graphs, models, specimens, films-strips, slides, museum cases and display cases. Among the important auditory materials may be included radio, tape recording, television and sound films. Auditory and visual equipment, such as projectors, recorders, radio and television receivers etc. may be housed in the library for use by the entire school. Many of these materials present information which is difficult to obtain through reading. They add realism and furnish the class with a common background of experience.

COLLATERAL READING AND THE LIBRARY

Collateral and supplementary reading forms and essential part of history programme. Students must collect a lot of information about various facts and movements after consulting many books and periodicals, besides their text-books for solving problems, doing assignments and participating ill discussions etc. Library resources can furnish a rich supply of books, periodicals and pamphlets for collateral reading. Text-book material must be supplemented by additional reference reading. Students should be encouraged to read Widely on topics of their own interest, both for the sake of information and entertainment. They should be guided how to select, read and make use of the knowledge thus obtained. They should be able to form good reading habits along with power study procedures. They should be encouraged to take notes and to keep a regular record of their reading.

LIST OF BOOKS AND OTHER INSTRUCTIONAL MATERIAL FOR HISTORY LIABRARIES

A. Books on Teaching of History

Aggarwal, J.C., Teaching of History: A Practical Approach. New Delhi, Vikas Publishing House Pvt. Ltd., 1992.

Beals, AC.F., A Guide to the Teaching of History in Schools. London,University of London Press, 1937.

Binning, A.C., and Binning, D.H., Teaching in Social studies in Schools, New York. McGraw Hill Book Co., 1952

Bloch, Marg,The Historian's Craft. Manchester University Press, 1959.

Brown, C.F., The history Room. London, Historical Association, Pamphlet No. 86, 1948.

Chaudhary, K.P., Audio-Visual Aids in Teaching Indian History Delhi, Atma Ram & Sons, 1965.

Chaudhary, K.P., Contents of History in Indian Schools. New Delhi, Ministry of Education, Government of India, 1953.

Chaudhary, K.P.,The Effective Teaching of History in India. A Handbook for History Teachers, New. Delhi, NCERT, 1975.

Chaudhary, K.P., Preparation of Lesson Notes. Calcutta, Bookland, 1955.

Dale, E., Audio-Visual Methods in Teaching. New York, Dryden Press. 1954.

Dobbson, D.P., A Handbook for History Teachers. London, Methuen, 1929.

Dymond, D., A Handbook for History Teachers. London, Macmilan, 1929.

Findlay, I.J., History and its Place in Education. London, University of London Press, 1923.

Ghate, V.D., The Teaching of History. Delhi Oxford University press, 1973.

Ghosh, K.D., Creative Teaching of History. Calcutta, Oxford University Press, 1951.

Gustavson, Carlg, A Preface to History. New York, McGraw Hill, 1955.

Hill, C.P., Suggestions on the Teaching of History Towards World Understanding. Paris, UNESCO, 1954.

Johnson, H.Teaching of History in Elementary and Secondary Schools. New York, Macmillan, 1942.

Knowlton, D.C., Making History Graphic. New York, Scribner, 1925.

Kochhar, S.K., Teaching of History. New Delhi, Sterling Publishers Pvt. Ltd, 1989.

Ministry of Education, Handbook of Suggestions for Teachers. London, H.M. Stationery Office, 1950.

Ministry of Education,Teaching of History. London, H.M. Stationery Office, Pamphlet No. 23, 1950.

National Institute of Education, Improving Instruction in History. Vol II, New Delhi, 1969.

NCERT, Teaching History in Secondary Schools. A Handbook for History Teachers. New Delhi, NCERT, 1970.

Pandey, B.N. and Khosla, D.N., Student Teaching and Evaluation. New Delhi, NCERT, 1974.

Srivastava, H.S. and Udin, Qamar,Sample Unit Tests in History. New Delhi, NCERT, 1982.

Vajrwswari, R. A Handbook for History Teachers. New Delhi, Allied Publishers, 1973.

B. Books on History

Agrawal, Ashvini., Rise and Fall of the Imperial Guptas. Delhi, Motilal Banarsi Dass, 1989.

Basham, A.L., The wonder that was India. London Sidgnick & Jack son, 1985:

Basham, A.L., The Indian Sub-continent in Historical Perspective. London School of Oriental and African Studies, University of London, 1954.

Bharatiya Vidya Bhavan, History and Culture of Indian People. Vols. I, Bombay, the Author.

Bose, M.L.A., Social and Cultural History of Ancient India. New Delhi, Concept, 1980.

Burke, S.M., Akbar the Greatest Mughar.New Delhi, Munshiram Manoharlal, 1989.

Carr, I.R., What is History? London, Macmillan & Company, 1961.

Chandra, Bipin, etc., Freedom Struggle.New Delhi, N.B.T., 1972.

Colling Wood, R.G., The Ideal of History. London, Oxford University Press, 1961.

Colling Wood, R.G., The Ideal of History. London, Oxford University Press, 1951.

Desai, A.R., Social Background of Indian Nationlism. Bombay, Popular Prakashan.

Dutt; R.C., History of Ancient and Modern India. New Delhi, Aribant, 1990.

Edwardes, Michael, History of India. New Delhi Asia Publishing House, 1961.

Goel, P.L., The Imperial Guptas. Varanasi Vidyalaya Prakashan, 1974.

Ghosal, H.R., An Outline History of the Indian People. Delhi, Publications Division, Ministry of Information and Broadcasting, Government of India, 1961.

Guide to Historical Literature

New York, Macmillan Company, 1931. (List of historical literature entire world).

Iswari, Parsad, Short History of Muslim Rule in India. Allahabad, The Indian Press Ltd., 1965.

Jain, Krishan Lal Hindu Raki in the World. Delhi, Akshat Pub., 1989.

Kosambi, D.D., Culture and Civilisation of Ancient India and Historical Outline. New Delhi, Vikas, 1989.

Kosambi, D.D., An Introduction to Indian History. Bombay, Popular, 1990. Kumar, Nirmal,The Stream of Indian Culture. Bombay, Bharatiya Vidya Bhavan,1979.

Lal, B.B. and Gupta, (Eds.), Frontiers of the Indus Civilisation. New Delhi Books and Books, 1989.

Law, D.A. (E.d.), Indian National Congress.New Delhi, Oxford University Press,l989

Mahajan, V.D., Ancient India. New Delhi, S. Chand & Co., 1989.

Majumdar, R.C. and Chopra, P.N., Main Currents of Indian History. New Delhi, Sterling Publishers Pvt. Ltd., 1979.

Majumdar, R.C. (Ed.), The History and Culture of the Indian People.Bombay, Bharatiya Vidya Bhavan, 1951.

Ministry of Information, India, Early History. New Delhi, Publications Division, Government of India, 1988.

Ministry of Information,India: Art and Architecture in Ancient and Medieval Period. New Delhi, Publication Division, Government of India, 1988.

Ministry of Information, lndia: People .New Delhi, Publications Division, Government of India, 1969.

Ministry of Information, lndia 1990. A Reference Mannual. New Delhi, Publications Division, Government of India, 1990.

Mukerjee, Radha Kamal, A History of Indian Civilisation. Bombay, Hind Kitab Ltd., 1956.

National Book Trust, Temples of North India. The Author, 1969. Nehru, Jawahar LaI, The Discovery of India, London, Meridian, 1951.

Nehru, Jawahar Lal, Glimpses of World History. Bombay, Asia Publishing House, 1936.

Pearce, F.G., An outline History of Civilisation. Bomaby, Oxford University Press, 1965.

Ramakrishan Mission Institute of Culture,The Cultural Heritage of India. Vols I-IV, Calcutta, The Author, 1958.

Sardesai, G.S., New History of the Marathas. Bomabay, Phoenix Publications, 1946.

Sarkar, J.N., Mughal Administration. Calcutta, M.C. Sarkar, 1962.

Sarkar, K.J.N., Fall of the Mughal Empire. Calcutta, M.C. Sarkar, 1949.

Sarkar, Sumit, Modern India. New Delhi, Macmillan, 1983.

Sastri, K.A.N. and Srinivasacharo, G., Advanced History of India. New Delhi, Allied Publishers, 1971.

Sastri, K.A.N., A History of South India. Bombay, Oxford University Press, 1966.

Sharma, S.R., Relgious Policy of the Mughals. Bombay, Asia Publishing House.

Singh Meera, Medieval History of India.New Delhi, Vikas, 1989.

Srivastava, A.L., Mugal Empire 1576-1803. New Delhi, Shiv Lal Aggarwal & Co., 1989.

Swain, J.E., A History of World Civilization. New Delhi, Eurasia Publishing House, 1983.

Tagore, Rabindranath, A Vision of India's History. Calcutta, Visva Bharati, 1963.

Tara Chand, History of Freedom Movement in India. New Delhi, Publications Division, Government of India, 1961.

Tripathi, R.P., Some Aspects of Mughal Administration. Allahabad, Central Book Depot, 1955.

C. List of Historical Atlases

Davies, Collins, An Historical Atlas of the Peninsula. Madras. Oxford University Press.

Fuller, H. and Trehana, R., Muir's Historical Atlas-Medieval and Modern.London, George Phillip and Sons Ltd., 1962.

Gilbert, Martin, Recent History Atlas 1870 to the Present Day. London, Weidenfold and Nicolson, 1967.

Kini and Rao, Oxford Pictorical Atlas of Indian History. Madras, Oxford University Press, 1973.

Parton, James., The American Heritage Pictorial Atlas of United States' History. 1966.

D. List of Biographical Historical Films

Title Black/White	Language	Duration	Call No.if any		Source
(1)	(2)	(3)	(4)		(5)
Abramh Lincoln (A Background Story)	B/W	E/H	15mm		U.S.I.S.
Abraham Lincoln (The force of)	B/W	E	22m		do
Abraham Lincoln (In Search of)	Col.	E/H	19m		do
Benjamin Franklin	B/W	E	20m		U.S.I.S.
Edison, Thomas Alva (Story of)	B/W	E	33m		U.S.I.S.
Galileo	B/W	E	14m	925	C.E.I.S.
Gandhiji	B/W	H	90m	923	C.E.I.S.
11 His memory We cherish	B/W	H	5m	923	do
Gandhi (Mahatma)	B/W	H	19m	923	do
Gandhi (Mahatma)	B/W	H	22m	157	A.V.L.
Gautam Buddha	B/W	E	90m		C.F.L.
Gorky R/W Russian With Sub title in English			110m	929.1	C.F.L.
J.L. Nehru (Our Prime Minister)	B/W	H	22m	723	C.F.L.

Contd.

(1)	(2)	(3)	(4)		(5)
J.L. Nehru (Life of)	B/W	H	35m	923.2	C.F.L.
Karve (The Story of)	B/w	H	21m	923	C.F.L.
Nobel Prize For Peace, Story (Workers for peace)	B/W	E	21m		U.S.I.S.
Netaji Subhas	B/W	H	150m		C.F.L.
Newton, Issac	B/W	E	10m	521.12	C.F.L.
Newton, Issac	B/W	E	13m	925	C.F.L.
Rabindranath Tagore	B/W	Pbi	22m	108.117	A.V.L.
Rabindranath Tagore	Do	H	22m	125	A.V.L.
do	Do	H	60m	920	C.F.L.
Ray, Pc (Acharya)	B/W	H	19m	925.4	C.F.L.
Theodore Roosevelt	B/W	E	20m		U.S.I.S.
Tilak, Lokmanya	B/W	H	22m	77	A.V.L.
Tilak, Lokmanya	B/W	H	20m	923	C.F.L.
Vivekanand (swami)	B/W	H	79m	922.44	C.F.L.
Life and Message of Vinoba Bhave: The Man	B/W	H	10m	923.2	C.F.L.
Washington, George	B/W	E	17m	927	C.F.L.
Washington, Irving	B/W	E	22m	970.22	C.F.L.
Wisweswaraya,	B/W	H	19m	920	C.F.L.
Woodrow Wilson	B/W	E	27m	–	U.S.I.S

E. List or Historical Films other than Biographical

Title	B/W Colour	Language If any	Duration	No.	Call Source
(1)	(2)	(3)	(4)		(5)
Ancient Egypt	B/W	E	10m	932	C.F.L.
Ancient Mesoptamia	Col.	E	11m	935	C.F.L.
Ancient World Inheritance	B/W	E	10ml	930	C.F.L.
Coast to Coast	B/W	E/H	30m	–	U.S.I.S.
Colonial Expansion	B/W	E	11m	970	C.F.L.
Dilli-Ki Kahani	B/W	H	65m	173	A.V.L.
English History: Civil War in England	B/W	E	33m	942.6	C.F.L.
English History: Earliest times to 1026	B/W	E	11m	942.00	C.F.L.
English History: 19th Century Reforms	B/W	Do	11m	942.05	C.F.L.
English History: Restoration and Glorious Revolution	B/W	E	11m	942	C.F.L.
English History: Stuart Britain	Col.	E	10m	942.06	C.F.L.
English History: Tudor Period	B/W	E	11m	942.05	C.F.L.
Evolution and	B/W	E	19m	177	A.V.L.
Hindu America	B/W	E/H	11m	970.1	C.F.L.
Ganga Ki Lahren	B/W	H	16m	959	C.F.L.

Contd.

(1)	(2)	(3)	(4)		(5)
Home Divided	B/W	E/H	30m	–	U.S.I.S.
Hundred Years	B/W	H	15m	571.954	A.V.L.
Immortal Stupas	B/W	H	13m	571.0954	C.F.L.
Indian Ocean	Col.	E	22m	942	C.F.L.
(Growth of the British Empire round the Indian Ocean)					
Cave Temples in India Pt. 1	B/W	H	10m	49	A.V.L.
Cave Temples in India Pt. 2	B/W	H	10m	50	do
Cave Temples of India Series, Buddhists	B/W	H	11m	726.193	C.F.L.
Citadels of	B/W	H	14m	176	A.V.L.
Chivalry (Forts of Rajasthan)	B/W	H	14m	954.52	C.F.L.
Industrial Revolution	B/W	E	11m	944.04	C.F.L.
Meaning of					
Indus Valley Civilisation	B/W	E	14m	954	C.F.L.
Indus Valley Civilisation	B/W	H	14m	154	A.V.L.
Jain Temples in India	B/W	H	16m	726.143	C.F.L.
Hill Temples of Gujarat	B/W		13m	726.143	C.F.L.
Malwa	B/W	H	11m	954.4L	C.F.L.
Man and his Culture	B/W	E	16m	901.9	C.F.L.
Mugal Glory Col..		H	19m	731.76	A.V.L.

Contd.

(1)	(2)	(3)	(4)	(5)
The Mughals do		E/H	22m 954.2	A.V.L.
The Mughals Col.		E/H	22m 90	A.V.L.
A Day in Mugal Times	Col.	E	14m 954.02	C.F.L.
Nalanda	B/W	H	10m 378	C.F.L.
Nation Rises: A	B/W	E/H	30m –	U.S.I.S.
A nation Sets Its Course	B/W	E/H	30m –	U.S.I.S.
Our Constitution	B/W	E/H	13m 954	C.F.L.
Page from History	B/W	Hindi	11m 91	A.V.L.
Page from History: A	Do	H/E	11m 954.7	C.F.L.
Pre-History Times (World before man)	B/W	E/H	11m 14	A.V.L.
Pre-History Times 11 11 (World before man)			11m 571.954	C.F.L.
Rajgir	B/W	H	16m 915.412	C.F.L.
Rajput Glory (Ancient Movements of Rajasthan)	B/W	E	11m 954.4	C.F.L.
Reformation	B/W	E	14m 940.23	C.F.L.
Renaissance	B/W	E	11m 940.21	C.F.L.
Rise and Fall of Nazi Germany	B/W	E	22m –	C.F.L.
Roman Episode: A Col.		E	10m 938	C.F.L.
Romances of Indian coin	B/W	E	11m 737.4	C.F.L.

Contd.

(1)	(2)	(3)	(4)		(5)
Romances of Indian coin	B/W	E	11m	172	A.V.L.
Seven Pagodas (Mahabalipurm)	B/W	H	11m	51	A.V.L.
Six years of freedom (1947-53)	B/W	E/H	13m	954	C.F.L.
Story of Pre-Historic Man	B/W	E	11m	171	A.V.L.
The New World	B/W	E/H	30m		U.S.I.S.
Thousand years of Gujrat	B/W	H	20m	954.46	C.F.L.
The True Freedom	B/W	E/H	30m	954.46	U.S.I.S.
Vijayanagar (Forgotten Empire)	B/W	H	11m	954.8	C.F.L.
World History	B/W	E/H	11m	900	C.F.L.
Yatree (Visit to Ajanta and Ellora Caves)	B/W	H	88m	954	A.V.L.

FILMSTRIPS

Name of the Title	Name of the Producer/Distributer
1. Bapu, the story of B/W	Producer: Almeryn Studio, Bombay, Distributor, Christian Association for Radio and TV, Jablpur
2. The Age of Exploration	Producer, EBF, USA; Distributor Photophone Pvt. Ltd.,
3. Pre-Historic Life	Producer, EBSS, U.S.A.; Distributor Photophone Pvt. Ltd.

4. Ancient Rome	Producer, EBF, U.S.A.; Distributor Photophone Pvt. Ltd., 7 Saki Vihar Road, Bombay.
5. Medieval Europe	do
6. Rise of Civilisation	do
7. Captain Cook	Producer Common Ground, London: Distributor, NEIE Appollo, Bunder, Bombay.
8. Christopher Columbus	do
9. Florence Nightingale	do
10. Pasteur and Microbes	do

HISTORY MUSEUM

On the role of school museums the secondary Education commission has observed, "Museums play a great part in the education of school children as they bring home to them much more vivdly than any prosaic lectures, discoveries of the past and various developments that have taken place in many fields of science and technology." Again the Commission observes, "We believe it is necessary from the educational point of view to establish such museums in important centres at least wherein both ancient and modern collection will be exhibited and in some cases even demonstration given of the actual process of development of various scientific discoveries. Nothing can impress students in the formative age so much as the actual visualising of these experiments in a graphic manner." History museums are made up or materials used in class-room teaching which are collected, classified and exhibited by students, with or without the help of a teacher. The museum activities may be an extracurricular function of the class or the school or they may be incorporated into a scientific-experimental method of teaching. Objectives: *(1)* To form within the school or the classroom an embryonic community dedicated to the usual occupations reflected in the school life of adults; *(2)* To permit Visual instruction and experimentation with actual museum speciments; *(3)* To stimulate enthusiasm for study and research among both teachers and students; *(4)* To stimulate interest, co-operation and participation in the cultural activities and scientific research conducted by the larger museums; *(5)* To insturct students in proper scientific methods of laboratory research and museum conservation and exhibition techniques; *(6)* To form, in the absence of larger museums in the community, a nucleus from which the class-room museum can grow beyond the limits of the school to serve ultimately the community and the region as whole.

Material to Improve Museum

(1) Dramatic Labels. In the museums or they are far too short. Large letters placed at the focal point of the case or exhibit area will successfully headline, the exhibit and catch the visitors attention like a news paper headline the main label tends to direct the eye smaller, less conspicuous letters that outline the most important points of the exhibit.

(2) Dramatic Lighting. Coloured lights that change, fade or highlight and exhibit can be used with great dramatic effect. Light can also be used to tell a story and to convey a sense of passing time.

(3) Dramatic Utilization. Museum visitors should be given a chance to feel exhibits as well as to see them but certain types of material-objects of wood, stone and metal and special "touch me" samples of animal skins and fabrics can be used with great success to satisfy the visitor's urge to touch while permitting a minimum of danger.

(4) Dramatic Sound Effects. Sound, like light, can be used to heighten the dramatic effect of visual communication. For example, an Amazon rain forest exhibition can be made vastly more effective by adding the sound of tropical rain, the croaking of frogs, the chatter of monkeys, and the beat of drums. An exhibit of medieval art can be made more meaningful if it is accompanied by music of the same period.

❐

4

Methods of Teaching History

Rousseau. In the second half of the eigthteenth century Emile of Rousseau laid the foundations of the methodology. He became the inspiration of forward-looking and progressive educators. Rousseau improved and enlarged idea of Comenius and others and put them into practice. In his chief educational work Emile, be begins with his accepted principle "Everything is good as it comes from the hands of the Author of Nature; but everything degenerates in the hands of man." Rousseau points out that there are three great teachers, 'nature, man and things."

Johann Heinrich Pestalozzi. He attempted to "psychologise instruction." He declared that education was a drawing out process and not a pouring in process. The basis of all education lay in the nature of the child. The methods of instruction must be sought and constructed to that end.

Comenius. The origin of modern methodology of teaching history may be traced ot 'great Didactic' on Johann Comenius who lived in the seventeenth century. He believed that all instruction should be carefully graded and arranged in a natural order. Teacher should appeal through sense perception to the understanding of the child. The work of Comenius, however, was buried beneath the sea of religious controversy and bigotry of his age.

Willhelm August Froebel and Johann Freederich Herbart. Disciples and followers of Pestalozzi, they developed elaborate systems of education. Froebel dealt largely with the Klindergarten stage. Herbart gave his famous 'Herbartian Steps' which cast a flood of light on existing methods and became the stimulators of various other movements in the field of education. Herbart condemned the rote method. He stressed comprehension and association. He presented the revolutionary, concept that the outcome of education was not the strengthening of the mental facuties but rather the building up of an "apperceptive mass" of ideas was very Herbartian theory and practice became popular in Germany between 1865 and 1885. Teachers and students from many lands studied at Jena, a centre of Herbartian teaching. By 1890, these ideas were brought to America where they received an almost universal acceptance.

The period of Herbartian influence, was transitional one. It prepared the way for newer better concepts of education by 1910. Herbartian system of education was generally criticised. It stressed the teacher and the formal procedure of teaching. The new theories of educational philosophy emphasised the pupils. Emphasis during recent years has been on individual instruction in the classroom but the socialization of the individual must not be neglected. Almost all modern methods and procedures can be used to promote both.

Method As End

There is no single road to successful teaching. As Dr. R. Vajreshwari puts it, "There are many roads-highways and by-ways, royal roads and narrow lanes, delightful paths and rugged and rough ones, functional and decorative." The choice of a suitable method by a teacher depends upon many factors such as learner, the nature of the subject and the topic, the facilities available and above all the attitudes of the teacher.

As the method of teaching arises out of the needs of a learning situation. It cannot be the same for all times all situations, nor can it be the same for all teachers and all subjects. A method is an instrument and should be regarded as such. It should play the role of willing servant rather than of a tyrannical master. It is a mean to and end and not an end itself. All methods are interconnected, by and large. A method is not a mere mechanical device for passing on facts and figures.

FLEXBILITY AND RESEARCH IN THE USE OF METHODS

According the Education Commission Report, "It has to be remembered that advances in classroom practice never occur on a broad front, with all the teachers and the schools moving forward in unison....But the work of the best teachers can be cripplied, if they are not permitted enocouraged and helped to go beyond the departmental prescriptions. The success of an educational reform will depend upon the good school or the good teacher is able to go ahead and the necessary supports are provided to the weaker institutions to introduce the reform gradually." The Commission observed. "In a modern society where the rate of change and growth of knowledge is very rapid, the educational system must be elastic and dynamic. It must give freedom to its basic units, the individual pupil in a school, the individual teacher among his colleagues and the individual school (cluster of schools) within the system to move in a direction or at a pace which is different from that of similar other units within the system being unduly hampered by the structure of the system as a whole. In this process the freedom of the teacher is the most vital, it is almost synonymous with the freedom of the school for the pupils can rarely be freer than the men and women who teach them.

CHARACTERISATIONS OF GOOD METHODS OF TEACHING

1. Love of Work. They aim at inclucating 'love of work.'

2. Efficiency. They aim at developing the desire to do work with the highest measure of efficiency of which one is capable. The motto of every school and its pupils should be 'Everything that is worth doing at all is worth doing well'—whether it be making a speech, writting a composition, drawing a map, cleaning the classroom, making a book rack or forming a quence.

3. Clear Thinking. They aim at developing the capacity for 'clear thinking' which distinguishes every truly educated person, "Whether a student is asked to make a speech in a debating society or to write an essay or to answer a question in history, geography or science or to perform an experiment, the accent should always be on clear thinking and on lucid expression which is a mirror of clear thought."

4. Participation. They provide numerous opportunities of participation in freely accepted projects and activities in which discipline and cooperation are constantly in demand.

5. Wide Range. They expand the range of students' interest. "We would urge all schools to provide in the time-table, at least one free period every day in which students may pursue their favourite hobbies and creative activities individually or in groups, preferably under the guidance of some interested teacher," recommended the Commission.

6. Application. They aim at providing opportunities to pupils to apply practically the knowledge that has been acquired by them. They Aim at transforming present bookish schools into "work schools" or "activity schools."

7. Intelligence. They are adapted to suit different levels of intelligence.

8. Cooperative. They balance the claims of individual work with cooperative or group effort. The training of emotions, attitudes and social capacities take place best in the context of projects and units of work undertaken cooperatively. The Secondary Education Commission has recommended that the teachers should be so trained that they are able to visualise and organise at least a part of the curriculum in the form of projects and activity—units which groups of students may take up and carry to completion.

9. Interest. They aim at the quickening of interest and training in efficient techniques of learning and study.

10. Training in Study. They train the students in the art of study. They train the students in the use of reference material such as the list of contents and index in books, the dictionary, the atlas, and reference books like the encyclopaedia.

SEVEN-FOLD DIVISION

1. Inspirational Methods. These are primarily based on high activity on the part of the instructor teacher. An examples giving a sermon to the students or to any group of learners.

2. Natural Learning Methods. In these learning takes place in a nutural way and planning for learning is not necessary. Learners are left on their own, with free and unplanned activity. Thus, the emphasis on learning activity is high, whereas it is low on planned experience and on cognitive inputs.

3. Expository Methods. In these cognitive emphasis is very high, while student activity and emphasis on exparience is low. An example is the lecture method in which the main emphasis is on imparting cognitive information to the learners.

4. Individualized Methods. These are known mainly through the popularity of programmed instruction. Their main characteristics is the guided search encoouraged by the instructor or the teacher. Programmed instruction, self-study, computer oriented instruction, case method, and prescribed experiments in science are examples of individualized learning in which the main emphasis is for each learner to learn at his own place.

5. Encounter Methods. Carl Rogers popularized the term 'encounter', although several other terms are used like T-Group, sensitivity training, interpersonal confrontation and so on. In these methods the main emphasis is on experience and learner activity on providing experience through confrontation or through encounter, and not through cognitive understanding. These methods are affective for change in basic behavioural patterns and developing new ways of looking at things.

6. Discovery Methods. These are high on all the three dimensions: learner activity, experience and experimentation by the learner, and cognitive understanding. Simulation primarily come under the category as also self-generated experiments in science. The main emphasis of these methods is on problem-solving and providing necessary framework to the learner is also able to learn the rationale and ligic of what he has done.

Generally speaking, method is the "process of planning, guiding, sharing and evaluating learning with a group of students." Method is the procedure which a teacher follows to make learning easy and effective. It is composed of several important steps logically and systematically arranged by the teacher. The teacher should find out effective ways of guiding pupils to learn and develop.

After deciding about the history syllabus for various grades of "what to teach", the teacher must decide about "how to teach" or the methods of teaching history. Method is a link between aims and objectives and results and values. It should always be in accordance with the requirements of the age of students, their stages of edcuation and their physical environments. It should never be streotype. It should be flexible and workable. Its success is judged by its results in terms of pupil growth and development. It leads to learning that is "interesting, easily acquired, functional and continuous", is the result of appling good methods teaching. However there is no single road to successful learning. "There are many roads-highways and by-ways: royal roads and narrow lanes, delightful paths and rugged ones." Similarly there is and endless variety of methods. So Every teacher has to choose a method that suits him or her best, in accordance with the nature of the subject the scope of the topic, the age and stages of the pupils and the facilities available.

1. TEXT BOOK METHOD

Text-Book method may be defined as "that teaching procedure in which the mastery of the text-book is the immediate objective.". This is the procedure which "revolves around the text-book just as another procedure might revolve around the problem or the project." However, within the limits of the text-book method, we may find good as well as bad teaching. Since the text-book is very widely used, it is highly desirable on the part of the teacher to utilize it to the best advantage of his pupils.

Advantages

1. Conscise and Up-to-date. Text-book is a very useful means of getting concise and up-to-date information. An oral lesson may become lengthy, complicated and unintelligible. In a text-book, the subject-matter is logically and systematically arranged for students. It provides the minimum essentials and enables them to work out problems and projects and also to pursue further discussion.

2. Meeting the Needs of Students. As text-book is written from the students' point of view, recognizing their limitations. It meets their requirements by the use of simple language, headings, subheadings questions, assignments, maps, charts, pictures and other illustrative materials.

3. Developing Study Skill. A text-book provides a common basis on which can be mastered the process of reading, analysing. Outlining and summarising. It furnishes a common laboratory to develop study skills. The student forms the habit of studying the text-book independently at home.

4. Accurate Account of the Subject. As text-book gives a reasonably correct account of the subject field area in an organised manner. It is very useful for the pupils. Its treatment is logical and systematic.

5. Reflecting and Establishing Standards. A text-book indicates what the teacher is required to teach and what the pupils are supposed to learn. It greatly effects methods and reflects and establishes the standards of scholarship. It furnishes a basis for specific assignments, problems and projects. The teacher can easily establish class as well as individual standards.

6. Suggesting Application of the Material. A text-book suggests application of the subject-matter, through assignments, drills, questions, projects and other activities.

7. Expanding and Limiting its Scope and Size, According to Need. A text-book can expand and delimit its scope, size and content according to the changing needs of education. It may lead and follow the educational process.

8. Basis of Almost all Other Methods. Almost all methods can be used with the text-book as a basis of study. Assignment procedure, story-telling and discussion method as well as activity procedures like the problem, project and unit method, may be used with the help of a text-book.

Disadvantages

1. Possibility of Errors. As the whole field of subject-matter is condensed and encompassed by an author in a text-book to meet the requirements of students, there is a possibility of errors of detail or interpretation. This defect can removed if the teacher is competent enough to correct errors and counteract prejudiced interpretations, especially in a subject like history.

2. Memorisation. Pupils generally memorise the text-book work for word and reproduce the same black and white at the time examination. They blindlly accept what is given in the text-book. They feel that it contains all the needed information and knowledge. However, an enriched scholarship on the part of the teacher can be suitable gurantee against this disadvantage.

3. Only Minimum Essentials. As text-book contains only a summary treatment of the subject-matter it does not give lively details and leaves a lot to be done by the teacher. Without his planning and direction the students cannot derive full advantage of the text-book.

4. Domination. Because of its definite and convenient subject-matter a text-book may dominate the entire procedure of teaching. The students and teachers may fall into the rut of covering a certain number of pages in routine procedure. They may accept anything and everything they find in print. This can be overcome by the utilization of other aids, besides the text-book.

The text-book procedure is undesirable if the teacher bases all of his teaching upon a single text-book. Sometimes the teacher or one of the students, reads the text-book in the class. Difficult words and sentences are explained by the teacher and other flows in reading and pronunication are removed. This may be a suitable procedure in language teaching but it highly objectionable in case of history. Only a judicious use of a history text-book should be made both by the teacher and the student. Text-book is not an end itself. It is only one of the means. In fact book method is not method of teaching history.

2. BIOGRAPHICAL METHOD

Carlyle Says, "the history of what man has accomplished in this world, is at the bottom, the history of the great men who have worked here." Biography is the story of life of a great man or woman in whom the society may be interested. History is taught through the Biographical method, as important events, turn around the lives of great individuals. To emphasis the noble deeds of great persons biographies are presented in a chronological order. It is believed that great men represent the times in which they live and work. They initiate great historical movements leading to changes in the existing social order. Such a preliminary study enables the pupils to understand the details of these movements at later stages.

Advantages

1. Simplicity. As compared to the history of a nation, tribe or movement, which is generally complicated life story of an individual person can be more easily taught.

2. Providing Natural Interest to Pupils. Young children are by nature, hero-worshippers. Interested in persons and in their history they lived and suffer with their hereos. Biography has great appeal from them.

3. Providing Motivation. As children love and worship the noble and adventurous deeds of their heroes, so they are naturally motivated to study those personalities. The facts, woven round those personalities become living and interesting for them.

4. Inclucating Social and Moral Virtues. History of noble characters of the creates a desire among children to the great like them. They begin to hate evil deeds and love deeds. Lives in great men incluate many social and moral virtues among students like fellow feeling, patriotism, nationalism, sympthy, truthfulness, charity and self-sacrifice.

5. Study of Social Life. Personality of a king, noble or despot, is the true index of the condition of his subjects. The life-story of a great leader, is deeply connected with the social condition, prevailing in his or her time. Thus biographics help in the study of society and even of government.

Disadvantages

1. Develops Hero Worship. Hero-worship was considered to be a great virtue in the days of Carlyle, but in our days it is not taken to be wholesome for the growth of young children. According to modern psychologists, the child's personality may have only a stunted growth under the towering personalities of great and women.

2. Undemocratic. The main agrument advanced against this method is that it is undemocratic. Instead of laying stress on society, it lays stress on a few great presonalities. This approach is based on the undemocratic distinction high and low; great and small.

3. No Continuity of Subject-Matter. Taught through biographical method history does not provide continuity of treatment. It is a piece-meal study of some great men of the past, without any link of suject-matter, as whole. No single individual, however, great he or she may by, can represent the manysided interests of the society, of that period.

4. World Movements cannot be Taught. While we teaching history of a particular period, round the lives of great personalities only we loss sight of the great world movements and forces which influenced makind as a whole.

5. Complete History cannot be Taught. There may be some periods in which there may not be a single person, really great while we are teaching the story of humanity. One may come across dark period in which little progress was made. Such periods cannot be taught through biographical method.

6. Great Men do not Represent their Times. It is not essential that great men represent their time because generally denied by their contemporaries greatness to such persons is bestowed only by the posterity. Since great men are generally far above the average humanity of their times, they are usually termed as "rebels" and "martyrs" and seldom "great," by people of their own times.

3. LECTURE METHOD

The lecture method "involves teaching by means of the spoken word." It is a formal talk by teacher. It may profitably be used at all stages with all classes, but its success will depend upon individual teachers. Primary school children have no patience to listen to long talks or lectures. Their interest can only be captured through interesting stories or questions and answers. As small children cannot remain passive listeners their interest should be aroused by means of questions and answers or interesting stories. But qustions at this stage should be related to their environment. Children also be encourage to put as many questions to the teacher as possible.

A good teacher does not take to much. He does not dominate the learning process. He assumes a major share of the responsibility for planning and guiding a number of activities, experiences and situations which result in functional learning for the group of pupils in his class. He selects the proper teachings to meet the needs, interests and capacities of his pupils at a particular times and particular situations. A lecture is a technique of description explanation and clarification. Effective and useful with young college students, it should also be useful with the same students only a year or two before they enter college.

Advantages

1. Immediately Repeated and Modified. Whenever the teacher feels that his talk is not being followed or appreciated by his pupils, his can repeat the ideas or expand and modify his statement. A sensible teacher would never like to "talk over the head" of his pupils.

2. Spoken Word More Effective than a Printed One. A spoken word is always more effective than a printed one. By his tone, gesture and facial expressed the teacher can indicated the exact sense or meaning which he wishes to convey. He can dramatise a scene, a story or a message; he wishes to give. Thus, his talk can have the colour and vividness which a printed book cannot have.

3. Time and Energy Saving. Because of their complicated nature sometimes facts of history are not clear to students in their text-books. Details are seldom given in text-books. Sometimes interpretations may also be wrong. The students may be lost in the maze of facts. They may spend a lot of their valuable time and energy in going through other sources for the clarification of such complicated points. A well-prepared and well-presented talk by the teacher is most helpful in that case.

4. Stimulating Students. As lecture demands of lot of preparation on the part of the teacher it advantages are transferred to the class as whole. Teacher's own preparation, his enthusiasm and his interest stimulate good students who may, like to persue projects, problems and other such activities in order to gain more and more knowledge.

5. Good Training and Experience in Learning by Hearing. In democratic countries schools train children for adult life so that as democratic citizens they may participate fully and effectively in affairs of national importance. Lecture and talks play an important part in one's adult life whether we lead or follow others. Children are to be prepared from the school stage. Hence occasional talks and interesting lectures should be arranged for all types of school children.

Aims and Objectives

1. To Supplement the Knowledge of Pupils. Whatever amount of study, the student may have done, there is always need of further additions of the subject-matter by the teacher due to his own reading and experience. This can be done through a talk or lecture on the topic, under study.

2. To Stimulate Students. In the beginning of a new topic or unit teachers can stimulate pupils by presenting the outstanding aspects of the events or movements or the achievements of significant persons in every simple and easy words. This will arouse interest among the pupils who will like to know more about that topic.

3. To Clarify Concepts. After memorizing certain facts from the books without understanding their meaning and importance the students are not helped in time they may, from wrong notions. Through an informal talk the teacher should correct such wrong notions and clarify the pupils' doubts.

4. To Prepare the Students to Undertake an Assignment, a Project or an Activity. It is always advisable to give an informal talk before any assignment or activity or project on group level is undertaken by pupils. This will save them from unnecessary wastage of time and energy in searching relevant material. It guide them to achieve the maximum in the shortest possible time and with minimum of labour.

Disadvantages

1. Ineffective. Teachers who do not know how to lecture in an effective way, cannot prepare and deliver well connected and relevant talks on topic given in the text-book. Lecture method will not succeed when used by such teachers.

2. Unnatural. Lecture Method is not a natural way for the pupils to learn. It makes them passive listeners. During the course of the talk, they may wander of to some more pleasant thoughts and may not attend to the talk at all.

3. Harmful Extensive Use. Thus, only occasional and informal talks may be desirable for realising definite purpose in view. If used extensively, the lecture method tends to substitute the teacher for the text-book.

4. Heavy Teaching Load. A teacher required to teach in the school right from the first period upto the last without break, is not expected to lecture in each period. He will not have the capacity to prepare so many simple and interesting lectures each day. It will not be physically possible for him to speak continuously for four or five hours a day.

5. Monotonous and Dull. Only exceptional teachers can stimulate interest through their talks at all grade levels. To avoid dullness and to give effectiveness to his lesson a successful is he who uses a variety of methods. If only the lecture method is used, the lessons may become dull and dry.

Teaching history through an informal talk or lecture is not the only method. It should always be accompained by illustrations, comparisons, charts, pictures, diagrams and other aids. Lecturing is an art, whose success depends on the teacher's depth of knowledge and his awareness of human factors, interest and motivation. A lecture is primarily meant to re-inforce key ideas and facts and to place them in a context of thought. It presents a philosophical whole out of a number of related fragments of information that can be obtained piecemeal by other means. It can not put together such information without the nature judgment and wisdom of a good teacher.

4. STORY-TELLING METHOD

Children, by nature, are very curious. Stories satisfy curiosity. The famous Greek educator. Plato laid stress on story-telling method for educating young children. Pupils in elementary and primary classes are fond of listening to stories. If the teacher tells them of the lives of great mean or how man lived in various ages, it arouses their interest and provides scope for imagination. In early stages of education, the subject matter should be so organised that it may look like a story.

1. Acting. He should have some elements of dramatic power, the art of acting, a keen sense of humour and a capacity for clear exposition.

2. Requirements. Interest the teacher should himself be intersted in the subject-matter of history.

3. Enthusiasm. He should have enthusiasm for the subject and be able to communicate his enthusiasm to children.

4. Order. While narrating stories, the teacher should keep in mind the chronological order and the sense of time and space.

5. Style. His style of narration should be natural, simple and interesting.

Types of Stories

1. True Stories. These have their unique place in history. They render valuable service in the effective teaching of history.

2. Myths. Their are stories which deal with fairies and other supernatural objects. As such they are false and of little historical value. These do not hold any importance in the teaching of history.

3. Legends. These do possess some element of truth though their details are generally not accurate. They be used in elementary and junior classes where accuracy of details, does not matter much. In the words of Prof Jarvis, "Truthfulness should be the major criterion to guide us in taking the help of stories, while teaching history. Historical stories, whether facts or legends, must be formulated by a truthfulness which is higher than were accuracy of incidents."

Advantages

1. Inculcating Good Virtues. In the words of Prof. Jarvis, "Story is adding in the formation of ideals of conduct and so it is contributing to the development of child's character and personality."

Life stories of great men and women inculcate virtues piety, truthfulness, valour, charity and leave lasting impression on the pupils' minds.

2. Enhancing Interest. Stories are the best means of arousing the interest of young children, especially in a subject like history.

3. Developing Imagination. Good stories develop the imagination of young children. In the age-group from 'six to eleven' young pupils love stories which are full of magic, wonder and adventure. These stories can provide ample scope for the development of pupils imagination.

4. Providing Inspiration for Creative Work. Effective story-telling inspires children for undertaking of creative work. From the very beginning they may be interested in making models of caves in which the ancient cave-men lived as model of stone implements which the cave-men used. They may also like to draw sketches of caves, implements and other things, used by their ancestors, thousands of years ago.

5. PROBLEM METHOD

It is a specific procedure by which a major problem is solved through the combined solutions of a number of smaller related problems. The problem method consists of the organisation of the school work to present to the learner a genuine problem that challenges him to a sustained effort to achieve its solution on mental plane. Problems in the class-room should originate from the suggestions by the teacher and the pupils working in cooperation. Teachers may take the entire course in history, in terms of one big problem. Units may also be taken as problems, which become sub-topics of one big problem. Class-room problems vary greatly in nature and complexity. The simplest may be in the form of an ordinary question whose solution involves only a little bit of factual knowledge. The difficult problem may be in the form of a unit like, "How the British traders became rulers of India." It solution involves the collection of material and facts from different sources for at least a couple of weeks or even more.

General Principles of Problem-Solving

1. Need Fulfilment. To arouse the curiousity of children for finding its solution the problem must include interest plus values. The children must feel it worthwhile to make efforrts for its solution, as it will fulfil their immediate need.

2. Selecting Material. The means of problem solving must not be vague to the pupils, otherwise most of the value of the procedure will be lost. Judicious solution of the material must be made. Material must be according to the age and capacity of pupils. It should also be easily available.

3. Definite Statement. After the pupils have come to feel the probelm as their own, the teacher must see that it is stated in definite terms. Defined clearly, the pupils will be able to keep it in mind while working on the references. They will be able to find out its solution without much difficulty.

4. Definite and Clear Solutions. Many means should be adopted to arrive at definite conclusions. One of the pupils should be asked to summarise the conclusion before the whole class. Then the other pupils should evaluate and criticise it unit. it is accepted by all. Definiteness of the conclusion or solution must be emphasised. The teacher, should help the pupils to apply the newly gained knowledge or skill to some immediate problem situations.

Advantages

1. Pupil's Activity. The pupils are stimulated to struggle for solutions of certain problems. They are no longer passive members of a class but active participants. They themselves make efforts to solve problems.

2. Life Conforming. Training in problem-solving will help the students to form certain attitudes and skills, so essential for adult life. It constitutes a realistic method for presenting the type of experience that will face the pupils throughout their career. They will be meet life situations with boldness, courage and success. Problem-solving will be a good preparation for solving personal and community difficulties in later by the pupils.

3. Critical Judgment. Because of self-activity involved in problem-solving Children become interested in their programme and develop the power of critical judgment. In a democracy where the success of a government depends upon the judgment of the people. this is of vital importance.

4. Initiative and Responsibility. As the pupils feel that the process is not a task assigned but an inevitable requirement of the situation, they get a chance to think, to judge and evaluate and to compare responsibility. It makes them useful and effective in adult life.

5. Assimilated Knowledge. Knowledge gained as a result of purposeful activity, connected with pupils everyday life is easily assimilated. It remains with the child permanently because it has been gained in real life situation.

6. Open-mindedness and Tolerant. As the pupils find that there are so many sides to a problem, they listen to different points of view, so they become tolerant in outlook and open-minded in their attitude. This attitude is very important in adult life these days.

7. Harmonious Relationship between the Teacher and Pupils. Teacher's guidance plays an important part in problem-solving. He has the ability to see problems clearly, the power to analyse with discernment and the facility to synthesise and draw conclusions with accuracy. He is a rare help in mastery of this difficult technique of problem-attack. He learns to appreciate the guidance of the teacher in helping them to achive their goal.

Disadvantages

1. Requires too Much Reference Material. Some problems require too much reference material which may not be available to students. Suitable books may also not be available in the school liberary.

2. Monotonous. If used too frequently this may become monotonous. If students continue working on one problem for days or weeks together, they lose interest in it. If one and the same activity is continued for many days or weeks, it must become dull and uninteresting.

3. Too Much Time Consuming. Preparation and initiation of the problem solving procedure may take a considerable portion of the teacher's time. As too much time of the class may also be consumed buy this procedure, it is not possible to make a continuous use of this method. The teacher has to cover a vast syllabus in history, in each term. This may not to possible if he takes to teaching by this method. One problem may take weeks or even months for its solution.

4. Not always Satisfactory Result. Satisfactory result are not achieved due to certain factors. If the pupils may become dissatisfied and discouraged. They may feel that problem-solving has been a sheer waste of time and energy. Such a feeling may develop wrong attitudes in them, like futility and cynicism etc.

6. DISCUSSION METHOD

Ours is an age of discussion. We arrive at definite conclusions and decisions after through discussion. Discussion has now come to challenge the authoritarian methods through which education was imparted in old days. In old days the teacher's authority was accepted in all matters. The pupils had little say in the instructional programme. Today the entire literary and non-literary activities, to be carried on, in and outside the class room, are first discussed in a socialized atmosphere by the teacher and his pupils and then given a practical shape. Discussion may assume the form of a conference, a symposium or a seminar. Once a subject is put to discussion, we cannot withdraw it, nor we can clothe it again with mystery. The main purpose of discussion is to educate young children in the process of "group thinking" and "collective decision."

Constituents of a Discussion

1. The Leader. The teacher is the leader of discussion. He prepares and conducts the discussion. He has do a lot of study, preparation, selection and planning. He must not dominate the entire scene because such an attitude will block rather than facilitate the "meeting of minds". He should be a co-worker and a co-sharer. He should watch carefully while the discussion is going on and act as a prompt guide, when the pupils are face to face with difficulties.

2. The Group. Students in a history class form the group. This group should be composed of all types of students including slow as well as quick leaners. The teacher should encourage every student to participate in the discussion.

3. The Problem. The problem or topic for discussion must be one which the students should feel their own. It should be made as precise and exact as possible. Its selection should be made by the teacher with the co-operation of his pupils. It must be real and functional and within the capacity and comprehension of the pupils.

4. Evaluation. At the end of the discussion each participation should evaluate whether discussion has added to his knowledge and information, changed his ideas, attitude and prejudices and increased the range of his interest. A successful discussion brings in the necessary change and makes the participation a more active than before.

5. The Content. The content is the body of knowledge. It is the needed material of study. It should include maps; charts, pictures, diagrams and other audio visual aids, Facts, cannot be discussed as these may not be proved true or false. But"statements about value." can be discussed and their truth established. Difference of opinion arises and discussion takes place about these statements.

Advantage

1. Collective Decision-Making. A Class-room discussion is an organised process of collective decision-making seeking agreement. It has the value of clarifying the nature of disareement.

2. Providing Knowledge. Participants in a discussion must possess definite factual knowledge. A number of arguments are given during the discussion. It adds to the participants. Issues are clarified and new grounds are disecovered for both agreement and disagreement.

3. Inclucating Toleration. There must be difference of ideas and understanding during discussing. Different people may believe in the same differently for different reasons. Participants in a class-room discussion must have patience to listen to different opinions and tolerate views are contrary to their own.

4. Intellectual Team-Work. Discussion represents a type of intellectual team-work, based on the principle that pooled knowledge of several persons is more advantageous than that of a single individual. This as a method of teaching history discuss is useful both for the junior and senior students although senior students are in a better position to collect and present information, make suggestions and share responsibility.

5. Self-evaluation. Discussion inolves a lot of thinking along the lines of self-evaluation. It establishes an attitude of looking forward to progress and growth.

7. PROJECT METHOD

A modern contribution to educational theory and practice is a result of John Dewey's philosophy of education and a natural extension of the problem method. The credit for initiating this method goes to professor William H. Kilpatrick, who has defined it as a whole-hearted purposeful activity, proceeding in a social environment." Dr J.A. Stevenson who perfected it as a method of teaching says, "A project is a problematic act carried to completion in its natural setting." Give me another definition Ballard says, "A project is a project which results in doing. The motor element is not what makes the activity a project, but the problem-solving of a practical nature, accompanying the activity."

This project method lays great stress on the actual action or activity on the part of pupils. Nothing is imposed upon them from outside not even from the teacher, Who takes upon himself the duties of an adviser and a guide. It is a reaction against dull monotonuous, purposeless and life-less-room teaching. The curriculum, content and teaching of techniques are considered from the child's points of view. 'Learning by living' is a better description of the project Method than 'lerning by doing'.

Basic Principles

1. The Principle of Activity. A child is active by nature. Opportunities should be provided to the child to be active and to do things for himself. The project method provides ample opportunities to pupils to think and plan things independently and then carry out the project in co-operation with others.

2. The Principle of Purpose. As it impresses upon pupils the way of doing things in the school. So they put their life and soul in the work.

3. The Principle of Experience. The child gains knolwedge through experience which, in turn, comes through some purposeful activity. As Project Method enables the child to work in groups he learns to co-operate with others and to share his interests and purposes. He gets valuable social experience in co-operation, character building, practical democracy and citizenship.

4. The Principle of Reality. Human life is itself a big project. Since education is a preparation for life, we must create real life situations in the school. In Project Method the pupils are provided with opportunities to exercise their powers in real life situations. Hence they feel genuinely interested in such activities.

5. The Principle of Freedom. The desire for any activity should be spontaneous. It should grow out of pupil's own needs and puposes. If the children are to gain real experiences they should be left to themselves in an atmosphere of freedom to choose the activity according to their capacities and powers and freedom to gain useful purpose as a result of that activity.

6. The Principle of Utility. The knowledge gained through activity must be useful and practical. Experiences obtained through projects ensure utility because they are carried out under natural conditions. As the method gives useful training and full satisfaction to pupils they feel that their efforts have not gone wasted because their activity must end in something concrete which is useful from educational point of view.

Steps in the Project Method

1. Choosing a Project. Only such a project should be selected as may satisfy some real need of the pupils and is for the good of all of them. They must feel that the project is their own. In the words of Dr. Kilpatrick. "The part of the pupils and the part of the teacher in most of school work depends largely on who does the purposing. It is particularly the whole thing."

2. Providing a Situation. A Project is never to be forced upon pupils. The teacher should to provide such as situation according to the interest and aptitude of the pupils which may give them a spontaneous urge to carry it out. Situation may be provided by conversation on different topics, discussions on pictures, buildings or cities, by telling stories or taking out children on excursions and educational tours and trips.

3. Planning. After a suitable choice has been made the next step is to prepare a plan for the execution of the project. After a good deal of discussion planning is to be done by the pupils under the guidance of the teacher, who offer suggestions. The entire plan should be put in black and white by the pupils project book before working on that plan.

4. Judging or Evaluating. After the completion of the project, the students should be asked to review their work. They should note down their mistakes, if any, and see whether they had proceeded, according to the plan. It is a sort of self-criticism which is a very important form of training and should never be neglected.

5. Executing. When the plan is ready the teacher should encourage the pupils to out it into practice. He should ask the pupils to assign duties and distribute work among themselves, according to their individual interests and capacity. Each child must the given some work to do, for the successful completion of the project. They should be asked to work in cooperation with one another till the project is complete.

6. Recording. The pupils should maintain a project-book in which they should put down a complete record of all the activities, connected with the project. This record will include the choice of the project, its planning, dicussions held, duties assigned reference and books consulted, information gathered, difficulties felt, experiences gained, guidance sought etc. Important points for future reference and guidance are also to be noted down.

Characteristics of a Successful Project

1. Maximum Activities. It should provide activities of various types suitable to pupils undertaking the project. It should be able to draw the best from them.

2. Usefulness. It must be individually and socially valuable and must have a practical aim.

3. Economy. The project should give the best of results in the shortest possible time and with the least possible expenses. It should not be expensive.

4. Best Experience. The project must fulfil some educational purpose.

5. Availability of Resources. The material connected with the project, should be readily available in or in the neighbourhood of the school. The pupils should be able to handle it without difficulty.

It should provide experience of a very high standard, including social contacts and character training.

Advantages

1. Based on the Laws of Learning. Project method works in accordance with the psychological laws of learning such as the law of readiness, the law of exercise and the law of effect.

(i) The law of readiness requires the child's mind to be ready for acquiring knowledge. The planning and selection of the project, prepares the child's mind for the work, he is about to do.

(ii) The law of exercise requires the child to practice what he has learnt. The law of effect requires that learning should be accompanied by happines and satisfaction. Project method is based not only on learning by doing but also on learning by living.

2. Economical. As the project is of the children's own choice and interest, it is done speedily. It gives best of results in the shortest possible time and with the least of wastage of money and energy.

3. Learning By Living. The actual doing of things gives effective knowledge. By actually doing achieving things in the project, the child gets pleasure and satisfaction. All this makes the study of history interesting and effective.

4. Training for Democratic Way of Life. As the pupils work in co-operation with one another for a common purpose they acquire foresight, power of judgement, independence of thought and action, initiative, responsibility, resourcefulness, tolerance, self respect etc.

5. Dignity of Labour. It upholds the dignity of labour as pupils are required to do all types work with their own hand, including manual work.

6. Correlation. Knowledge is gained as a whole is its natural setting. All the subjects are correlated and there is no isolation of learning in water-tight compartments.

7. No Cramming and Memory Work. As it does not come as the finished thought-product of the teacher learning is effective. It comes as a by-product of useful activity. Children learn by doing things themselves. They learn the problem solving attitude and exercise thinking and reasoning power.

8. Education According to Real Conditions of Life. The projects are related to everyday needs and experiences of the child. As various subjects are taught to the extent, they are applicable in practical life, knowledge gained is real, practical and useful, leading to the formation of proper habits and attitudes.

Disadvantages

1. Too Much Strain on the Teacher. Project method expects too much of the teacher. Every teacher cannot be efficient in all subjects, nor so intelligent and resourcesful as to suggest suitable projects and impart knowledge through them in a correlated manner.

2. Haphazard and Scrappy Knowledge. The project method disturbs the logical and chronological arrangement of teaching history which is so essential. Losse ends of knowledge and left here and there, if work in different subjects is done according to this plan. Certain portions of the subjects do not come into the project at all.

3. Expensive. For its successful completion this method requires a lot of material. Which may not be easily available locally. Therefore ordinary schools can not afford to adopt this method as they are not in a position to spend so much project requires a lot of money material and time, which can be seldom snatch out of busy school programme.

4. Lack of Suitable Text Books. Suitable text books of history written on project method lines, are also not available. This adds to the difficulties of the teacher.

5. Disrupting School Work. If the school is to be run on project method is not possible to follow any fixed time table in the absence of any fixed curriculum, the precribed syllabus in various subjects is seldom finished in time. It is possible only if usual procedure of teaching is followed.

6. No Balanced Learning for All Pupils. Some more developed and capable children are inclined to take all the responsibility upon themselves. Keeping others in the background they want to do all the work. This provides ample opportunities to shirkers to look on and do very little. All the pupils are not expected to engage themselves in activities with equal seriousness and zeal.

8. SOURCE METHOD

The study and use of original material and original sources give a much better understanding of subjects like history than any other method. This is called the Source Method of teaching and learning history.

Classification of Sources

Historical sources are "traces" left behind in the past, by men. A historian tries to construct a systematic account of the past event with the help of such sources. Historical sources are classified as follows:

1. Archaeological sources
2. Literary sources
3. Oral tradition.

1. Archaeological Sources

(i) ***Monumental Finds.*** Buildings, images pottery and terracotta figures and other antiquities are monumental finds. The Archaeological Department of the Govt. of India has exacavated a large number of sites at various places in India, By which considerable material of historical value, has been brought to light with the help of his material, the historians have reconstructed the history of ancient and medieval India. Ancient buildings, sculptures, paintings, potteries and terracotta figures, throw light on the type of civilization of the period, to which they belong.

(ii) ***Numismatics.*** Old coins are very helpful in reconstructing ancient history. The extent of the kingdoms of particular ancient Indian kings, the length of their regions and the succession of different rulers of the same dynasty, are known through these sources. Coins also throw light on the economic and religious conditions of their times.

(iii) Epigraphics. Consisting of inscription on stones, pillars, rocks, copper-plates, bricks, seals, terracotta and images these source give us concrete evidence for the various phases of Indian history. India is very rich in such authentic sources.

2. Literary Sources

(i) Sacred or Religious Literature. In Indian this includes the four Veds which decribe the social and political life of the Indo-Aryans. The kalpasutras are manuals of rituals and also throw light on the development of sciences of Geometry and Architecture in ancient India. The Ramayana and the Mahabharta and the Puranas throw sufficient light on the social and political conditions of the Aryans settled in northern India as well as the history of several dynasties. The sacred literature, includes the Tripitakas, the Buddhist cononica literature and the twelve Aningas and the Jain canonical literature.

(ii) Foreign Accounts. The accunts of foreign tavellers to India also form an important source of Indian history. These include the accounts of Greek writers like Herodotus, Nearchus and Megasthenes, the Chinese pilgrims like Fahien, Hieun Tsang and Itsing and the Arab scholar, Alberuni.

(iii) Secular Literature. It includes novels, dramas, poems, books on medicine, grammar and astronomy, biographies, autobiogrphies, travellers, accounts, personal diaries and official orders and despatches. Examples are Shakuntala of Kalidasa, Mudra Rakshasa of Visakhadatta, Artha-shastra of Kautilya, Ashtadhyayi of Panini, Babar Nama of Babar, Tuzak-i-Jahangir; of Jahangir, Akbar Nama of Abul Fazal, Queen's Proclamation of 1858 and official despatches of various Governors and Viceroys, treaties and official reports.

3. Oral Tradition

Oral tradition is very helpful for local history. The noble deeds and heroic exploits of local heroes may not be mentioned in a general history of India but they live on in the oral form. Tod's Annals of Rajasthan, are mostly based on local tradition. For the reconstruction of the earliest history of India, we have to depend on the tradition of the ancient tribal people found only in and oral form.

Primary and Secondary Sources

1. *Primary Sources.* Also called original sources these include the accounts, prepared by those persons who were directly connected with an event or were the eye-witnesses to it, like official orders, treaties, laws, autobiographies and personal memories.
2. *Secondary Sources.* There are prepared by those persons who were not directly connected with the actual happening but who prepared their accounts with the help of eye-witnesses, like standard historical works, based on original accounts. As some of these might have been based on personal prejudices of bias, the teacher should select and use them very carefully for class-room purposes.

Methods of Utilising Sources

1. Assigned Reading. By assigning selected passages to be read by selected students the teacher can introduce the use of source. The selected passages should be interesting and immediately connected with the topic in hand.

2. Demonstration. By giving a demonstration of how to utilise them a teacher who believes in the utility of sources can best convince his pupils. He can do so by reading a particular passage from the original source, supporting or illustrating his point or throwing additional light on his opinion. He should make it quite clear to his pupils that source material is to be employed at appropriate times rather than to be read for the sake of reading. This will motivate his pupils to go through some such sources for clarifying certain controversial issues or for arriving at truth about a certain point.

3. Problem Solving. Problems can best be solved with the help of sources. With their help the pupils will be able to discover and correct errors in the text-books and in other secondary accounts if any. Source method is of great help and advantage to reach the truth.

Difficulties in Utilizing Original Sources

1. Sources of Real value not Available. In India efforts have not been made to edit and compile source books, suitable for school students. Original sources of real worth, suitable especially for school students, are too scanty and too disjointed.

2. Difficulty of Language. Almost all the original sources of historical or cultural value are in languages, foreign to Indian students. Indian pupils in schools cannot be expected to deal with long passages on English, Sanskrit, Pali, Arabic or Persian, the language in which most of the original sources are available. Relevant and short extracts from contemporary documents in the pupils' mother tongue can serve the desired purpose and these are seldom available.

3. Conflicting Views of Different Contemporary Writers. A source is not reliable only because it is a source. Like all other writers, source writers also have their own prejudices, faults, preference and limitations. Authors of different sources give different accounts of events or movements during the same period according to their own points of view.

Advantages

1. Giving a Sense of Reality. The use of sources gives a sense of reality. If properly handled and utilized, source accounts enrich and supplement the text book account.

2. Revealing the Nature or Reliable Evidence. Students using source, begin to realize the difference between a guess and assertion, between the exact words, spoken or written by a person and what someone else has said about that person's statements. Thus, they gather reliable evidence.

3. Providing Functional Knowledge. Handling original sources even the slow and backward children feel interested. Gained in the proper context their learning becomes functional. It arouses their curiosity, stimulates their creative expression and develops skills.

4. Affording Training in Reasoning and Judgement. The use of the source develops one's critical faculty of reading, thinking, reasoning and judgement. It teaches a person to examine carefully before arriving at final decision. The application of this valuable training can be transferred profitably to other situations in one's life.

9. UNIT METHOD

Today unit has become the most popular form of organisation in the teaching of history. Different ways of teaching history are designated collectively as the Unit Method. The extensive use of the unit Method of teaching in history followed the introduction of problems and projects. Unit method incorprates the use of both these earlier procedures. Contrasted to lesson-planning in terms of daily work, the unit procedure indicates plans of work to be done over a period, ranging from several days to many weeks.

Hanna, Hageman and Potter. "A unit can be defined as a proposeful learning experience, focussed upon some socially significant understanding which will modify the behaviour of the learner and enable him to adjust to a life situation more effectively."

Thus unit is an instructional device having significant content, involving pupils in learning activities through active participation and modifying the pupils' behaviour to the extent they are capable of coping with new problems and new situations. A circut is designated focus attention on significant results and to avoid the confusion and discouragement coming from long attention to non-significant details. Various events and movements are not to be taught in isolation in history. The vast subject-matter of history has to be organised in larger divisions. Each such division is called a Unit, "the organisation of material in related groups, each large enough to be significant but small enough to be seen as a whole by the pupils." The unit may be a subject-matter unit or an experience unit. It is "an organised body of information and experiences, designated to effect significant outcomes for the learner." New interests, new attitudes, new skills, and new ideas characteristics of a genuine unit.

Principle of Formation of Units

1. Due consideration to class, grade and time be given while forming units. Units for lower classes should be shorter than those meant for higher classes.
2. A unit must be comprehensive enough so that sufficient material may be available for its complete understanding.
3. Children's needs, interest, capacities and capabilities should be kept in mind while selecting units for them. They should not be big enough to confuse children with factual material. They should, rather, centre round the children's expanding interests.
4. A unit must have relationship to the whole course.
5. A unit should provide for the intellectual, social and emotional development of children, through the integration and correlation of their learning activities.
6. A unit should be evolutionary and functional, moving towards some definite goal.
7. A unit should be further split up into sub-units for the sake of clarity. For example, the unit "How British traders became rulers of India" may be divided into the following sub-units:
   (i) Early European settlements and emergence of the British as the leading power.
   (ii) Decline of the Mughal Empire.

(iii) Rise and Fall of the Marathas.

(iv) Rise and Fall of Hyder Ali & Tippu.

(v) Rise and Fall of the Sikhs.

Advantages

1. Variety of Outcomes. Well planned and skilfully executed, the unit procedure gives a variety of outcomes such as the extension of knowledge. The development of skills, abilities and attitudes etc.

2. Development of Traits. The traits that history teachers wish to develop in their pupils, are promoted through the units procedure. Among the important traits are cooperation, courtesy, leadership, loyalty and respect for good workmanship, opportunities for reading problem solving, project work, discussion and personal interviewing etc.

3. Flexibility for Adopting Instruction to Individual Differences of Children. Not aiming at fixed and uniform standard of achievement for all pupils unit method focuses attention on the individual child his problems and his interests. In case of different children unit keep different standards of achievement in order to meet the educational needs of individual pupils. This makes learning functional is units are based on the needs and interests of different types of children.

4. Natural-situation for Teaching Skills. In order to enable children to learn how to work in groups, it is essential that group situations be provided. This is possible through the unit-procedure which provides such situations. Development of socialization skills is basic to unit work. Opportunities are provided for development of these skills.

5. Effective Use of Supplementary Materials. In the unit a well-planned unit stimulates the use of textbooks, sources books, encyclopaedias, literature, pamphlets and periodicals etc. and many other types of supplementary material.

6. Democracy in the Class Room. This unit procedure examplifies democracy as an ideal in the class-room. Democracy is not only taught in spirit also be made the subject of the unit of study.

7. Progressive Measures in Teaching-learning Process. The unit method combines progressive measures like curriculum, correlation, fusion and integration and aslo encourage them.

Disadvantages

1. Insufficient Training. At present history teachers have not sufficient training in the technique of forming units and putting them into execution. It may be due to the nature of teacher training programme in training institutions and due to the lack of sufficient textbooks, periodicals, pamphlets and other supplementary materials.

2. Confusion. Unless pupils are taught by the unit procedure in all school subjects, they become confused when it is used only in one subject, namely, history, such a lack of uniformity in teaching methods, leads to a general state of wonder, confusion and indecision.

3. Failure in Learning Certain Basic Facts. Many of the fundamental facts of history are never learned through the unit plan. Specific characters, dates, places and technical vocabulary are liable to be easily over looked.

4. Unsympathetic Attitude of Visitors and Parents. Visitors or parents do not understand that noise, accompanying actual work, is justified in this procedure. They often feel that the classwork is all confusion and without any substance.

10. HEURISTIC METHOD

Spencer wrote, "Children should be told as little as possible and induced to discover as much as possible." In the heuristic method developed by Prof. Armstrong.The extreme application of this dictum is to be found. The first used in the teaching of science it was later on adopted in the teaching of all subjects in the curriculum. The word 'heuristic' comes from the Greek work 'heurisco' or 'heuriskein' which means to find out'. Hence the heuristic method is the method in which children find out things for themselves and are placed in the position of discoverers or inventors. It is the method of nature advocated by Rousseau in his 'Emile'.

Objective Method

In the words of Ryburn, "The object of teaching by the hesuristic method is not so much to teach facts... as to teach how knowledge of facts may be obtained, of how they can be systematised and of how they may be used. Pupils, who are taught in this way learn to be observant, exact and to think for themselves." It aims at developing scientific and critical attitude and spirit in the students. The object of the heuristic method is "to make pupils more exact, more truthful, observant, thoughtful and dexterous, to lay the solid foundation for future self-education and to encourage the growth of a spirit of enquiry and research."

Principle

1. Principle of activity or learning by doing.
2. Principle of experience.
3. Principle of freedom.
4. Principle of play-way.
5. Principle of purpose.

It awakens a spirit of enquiry through observation and fact finding. It utilises the instinct of curiosity of the children and prompts them to find facts through their own efforts. The children work in an atmosphere of freedom and in a play-way spirit.

The children are not mugging up certain facts. As they have to exert themselves learning becomes meaningful to them.

Advantages

1. It develops a scientific and critical attitude of mind.
2. It arouses the spirit of enquiry.

3. The students learn the art of planning their programmes.
4. The students learn facts through their own labour and therefore, retain them much longer.
5. It develops habits of hard work among by keeping the students busy to find out the requird solutions.
6. It fosters self-activity in the students.
7. It helps to develop the power of initiative self-confidence and self-reliance among the students by encouraging them to draw their own conclusions through their own efforts.
8. It help to develop good relationship between the teacher and pupils and among pupils themselves.
9. As the students remain busy in their work the problem of discipline is solved.
10. The fear of the home task disppears. The students are not to memorise facts at home but to find facts in the classroom or the laboratory.
11. It provides enough training to the students to prepare themselves for life. The students learn how to handle different situations and how to arrive at certain conclusions. The experience helps them in later life.
12. The students feel the pleasure and joy of achievement and sense of originality.

Limitation

1. As pupils are immature and one cannot put them in the position of discoverers or inventors.
2. As it is a very slow method it is not possible to finish the curriculum in time.
3. It requires teachers enthusiastic resourceful and hard working, of such teachers are scarce.

4. It is not suitable for primary classes.
5. It cannot be used at all occasions and all the time. On numerous occasions it becomes absolutely essential for the teacher to give direct information.
6. As it involves a close supervision on the part of the teacher, it cannot be used in large classes.
7. One cannot expect all the children to become discoverers and inventors because there are many children who are mentally deficient.
8. There is a great shortage of textbooks written on heuristic lines method.
9. Possessing a social heritage the child has every right to make full use of it. It is foolishness to make him repeat all the mistakes and hardships of the race. The heuristic attitude should pervade all teaching in the classroom. Better and quicker results will be achieved if the teacher is successful in maintaining this attitude.
10. Wrong generalisation may be arrived at. A lot of time and energy may be wasted.

❐

5

Teaching of Dramatization and Excursions

In dramatization, the actors assume to play the role of others. For example, if the life of Shivaji in enacted, the actor who plays the role of Shivaji, enacts not his deeds but those of Shivaji.

Elements of Learning by Doing

In teaching, 'activity' is very useful. It helps to provide stable knowledge. In dramatization, the students learn by doing and so their experiences are strengthened. This is what Prof. John Devy had said in the following lines:

"When a pupil learns by doing, he is relishing both—mental and physical experiences which have proved important to the human race."

Importance of Dramatization

Children are very active. The cannot sit idle. Dramatization can bring about proper utilization of their knowledge and activity. In dramatization, the basic instinct of the children *i.e.*, copying or acting according to others is satisfied. Prof. C.H. Jarvis has aptly observed, "It is sometimes assumed that children are born-actors and have a dramatic instinct; their attempts to dramatize story must naturally be successful and have an educational value, but a child's dramatic instinct is essentially initiative. A very young child will often do something quite spontaneously in imitation of another's action. Through imitation, it is possible to satisfy the instincts of activity and imitation of the children."

Development of Creative Instinct

Through dramatization, it is possible not only to develop the instincts of activity and imitation but also creatveness of creation.

Elements of Play

Drama also contains elements of play. In this process, children acquire knowledge while playing. According to the psychology, this is a very good method of imparting education to the children of tender age.

Elements of Dramatization and History Teaching

On account of the advantages enumerated above, dramatization is quite helpful in the teaching of history. In history, the students are taught about lives and deeds of different individuals which belong to different periods of history. In history, events and the factors responsible for these events are also taught to the students. It is, therefore, quite helpful for the teaching of history.

Types of Dramatization

Dramatization may be of the following two types:

(1) Extempore Dramatization. In this type of the dramatization, no preparation is made for it. It helps the children to develop the power of thinking and reasoning besides memorising what they have been taught.

(2) Prepared Dramatization. In this types of dramatization, preparation is made beforehand. Students are taught to speak out dialogues and act according to a certain pattern. This helps the students to acquire the habit of learning things. Although it is not helpful to extreme power of dramatization but it does help to some extent.

Precautions in the Dramatization

If technique of dramatization is to be employed in the teaching of history, the following precautions must be taken:

(1) The teacher should select a particular topic or event that has to be taught in the classroom. Preparation should be made with the help of the students.

(2) Students should be made to write dialogue and prepare them.

(3) The teacher should help to make the students prepare dialogues about the historical events and prepare them. This would help them to develop the power of writing from the material they have learnt.

Advantages of the Method of Dramatization

The element of dramatization is quite helpful in the teaching of history. It has the following advantages:

1. It provides them an opportunity to acquire knowledge through activity.
2. It has to develop the power of self-creativeness and activity.
3. It is psychological to help in developing the power of the learning of the students.
4. It provides a change to the students from the formal and rigid atmosphere of classroom and reading of books.
5. It also helps them to develop the power of sympathy and imagination.
6. It also broadens their outlook.
7. It provides education along with precaution.
8. The students develop the art of speaking while developing self-confidence and the power of understanding.

9. In the lower classes, it is easy to teach the history of students through this method in an effective manner.
10. It also develops in the students the power of appreciation and aesthetic sense.
11. Through, dramatization, several sense organs of the students get to work. They also develop.
12. Power of observation also develops through this method.
13. It helps in development of power limitation and also provides moral education in a suitable and interesting manner.

Limitations of Dramatization

It is not easy to apply the technique of dramatization in teaching of history always. It has the following limitations:

1. **Apprehension of Indiscipline.** While dramatization is going on, it is not possible for the teacher to maintain of rigid discipline in the classroom. There is, therefore, fear of indicipline.
2. **Lack of Knowledge in the Art of Dramatization.** Dramatization requires some technical knowledge. Every teacher does not possess it. This technique should, therefore, be employed only by those who have some knowledge about it.
3. **Dearth of Historical Events Fit for Dramatization.** All the events of history are not fit for dramatization. Teacher has, therefore, to select such events in a proper manner.
4. **Difficult Enacting.** Certain events of history are difficult to enact. For example, it is difficult to enact successfully the scene of war.
5. **Economic Factor.** Implementation of the technique of dramatization requires money. Several institutions are not

rich enough to provide so such of money for the teaching of one subject.

6. **Problem of Dialogues.** In employing this technique, it is necessary to have good dialogues. Writing of good dialogues requires aptitude as well at time. It is not possible for every teacher of history to do it successfully.

7. **Time Factor.** Dramatization is a time consuming teachique. It it not possible for school administration to spare so much of time for one particular subject.

8. **Dearth of Aptitude of Acting.** It is not possible to get good actors among the students easily. Every student is not necessarily a good actor, as is the case with the teachers.

In spite of all these limitations, dramatization is a good technique for teaching of history. It is quite useful in lower classes. It can be used in higher secondary classes as well, and that too, in a successful manner. The students of higher secondary classes are quite grown up and they can provide the things required for successful dramatization of an event. It higher secondary classes, the technique of dramatization should be used but with great caution.

Suitable Topics for Dramatization in Indian History

After discussing the dramatization method and its merits and limitations, it is also essential for us to point out some of the topics of Indian history that may be selected for dramatization. They are as the following:

1. The life of Buddha.

2. Alexander's invasion over India with special reference to the battle with Porus.

3. Prithvi Raj and Sanyogita.

4. Akbar and his Nine Jewels.

5. Rana Pratap after the battle of Haldighati.
6. Shivaji's escape from Agra.
7. The Revolt of 1857.
8. Dandi March of Mahatma Gandhi.
9. The proclamation of Indian Independence.

HISTORY TEACHING AND EXCURSIONS

Before 19th century, it was not thought necessary to make the teaching of history interesting. It was considered to be a dry and dull subject. With the development of latest thinking in the field of education, it was felt necessary to make the teaching of history quite interesting and real. This thinking has influenced and changed the mode not only of teaching of history but other subjects as well. It is now realized that to confine teaching of history within the four walls of the classroom, is not very wise. Teaching of history should be conducted at places of historical importance. With this realization, excursions have become an integral part of the teaching of history. The main aim of the teaching of history, with the help of excursion, is to make it realistic and interesting.This is what Prof. Henry Johnson has said in the following lines:

The school excursion, as envisaged by Prof. P. Reain, was prized for reality which is imparted to geography, nature study of history and other subjects. It was also prized for open air exercises which it brought for open air exercises which it brought for the initiative and freedom it made possible for the opportunity. It treated for social training.

Education Imparted Directly has a Lasting Value

Direct education is that which is acquired by the students themselves with the help of their different sense organs. Through excursion, it is possible for them to acquire education directly. In fact, excursion is an attempt at direct education of history.

Historical Excursions

For the teaching of history, excursions may be arranged to the following places:

1. Old forts, battle-places, monuments, etc.
2. Historical museums, collections of old historical arms, utensils, dresses, relics, coins etc.
3. Places of historical importance having historical ruins such as Fatehpur Sikri, Nalanda etc.
4. To monuments, tombs, places, caves, etc., having historical importance, such as Sikandra where the tomb of Akbar is situated, Tajmahal at Agra, caves of Ajanta and Ellora etc.
5. Things of historical importance.
6. Places where historical excavations have been carried out such as Mohanzodarao, Harappa etc.

Importance and Utility of Excursions in the Teaching of History

In the teaching of history, excursions occupy an importance place. In the modern days, they have become an integral part of the teaching of history. They make the teaching of history interesting as well as realistic. Following are the advantages of the excursions in the teaching of history:

(1) It Makes the Classroom Teaching of History Interesting. Teaching of the subject in the classroom is formal and dry. It does not provide any opportunity either to the teacher or to the students to display their aptitude and interests. There are limitations for the teacher and so he can make teaching of the subject interesting only within those limitations.

Excursions provide an opportunity to the students to go to open plces and have full advantaged of the opportunity of acquiring knowledge directly. This opportunity is utilized by the students to grasp things more easily.

They also acquire knowledge without having to undergo formal discipline of the classroom. Excursions, therefore, make the classroom teaching interesting. It is also possible for the teacher to keep the interest of the students alive in the subject after having brought them back from excursion.

(2) Development of Love for Culture Heritage. Through excursion, it is possible for students to acquire knowledge about the achievements of the their forefathers. They also know about their cultural hertiage. When they have a look at historical buildings and places, they remind of the great deeds of their forefathers. This thing fills them with love for he achievements of their for fathers and love for their cultural heritage.

(3) Development of Sense of Patriotism. The main task of education and the teaching of social sciences is to develop the students into ideal and patriotic citizens. The objective is fulfilled by taking the students to places of historical importance. When the students have a look at these places of historical importance, patriotism is aroused in them.They feel pride for their mother land.

(4) Development of the Knowledge of Local History. Through excursions, it is possible to impart to the students knowledge of material, social and historical facts. It is also possible to explain to them the relationship between the economic and social phenomenon. It also helps them to acquire knowledge that shall be helpful for their day to day life.

(5) Development of Mental Faculties and Powers. Excursions provide students with the opportunity for observation, imagination and research. Such an opportunity bring about development of their mental faculties, thinking, reasoning and appreciation of beauty etc. That is what the real education is.

Planning of a History Excursion

It is an old saying that "Well begun is half done". This is true about historical excursions as well. If a particular historical excursion has been properly planned, its object is more or less fulfilled. Following considerations have to be kept in mind while planning a historical excursion:

1. A pre-survey of the historical material should be conducted before the excursion is planned to that place.

2. If the teacher has to take his students to certain historical places, he should equip himself with full knowledge about those place. It is possible that while the students are going round that place, they may put several questions about that

3. The place of excursion should be properly settled. There should be no element of uncertainty or indecision once has been done. Following things should be determined:

   (a) The aim of excursion should be properly determined. While determining it, the cooperation of the students should be sought.

   (b) It should also be kept in mind that while developing the aim, the students should acquire a good deal of educational experiences. A programme in this regard should also be drawn up beforehand. While the journey is performed this programme should be kept in mind and carried out as far as possible.

   (c) The students should be told that they have to carry with them note book, pen or pencil, camera is possible, bedding, clothes that small stand the strain of the journey.

   (d) In the excursion, students should be divided into different groups and each group should be entrusted with one responsibility. This division of labour shall, on one hand, facilitate matters and on the other, it shall make the excursion successful.

   Apart from fulfilling the objective, such a division shall also help the students to develop the quality of leadership.

While the students are being taken on excursion, they should be guided properly. Their questions should be properly answered.

4. The students should be asked to make notes. These notes may be latter on used in the classroom.
5. Excursion should not be confined to the places of historical importance. Attempts should also be made to come into touch with the people of those places. Such a contact will provides the students with more informations about the historical facts of the places.
6. While the students are being shown the things of historical importance, such as a tomb, teacher should throw light on all possible details about that thing. For example, if the students are being shown the Red Fort of Delhi, they should be told all the historical facts about it.

If the teacher gets an opportunity to sit with the students in a group while on excursion, after he has shown them some historical things, he should try to make them discuss about the things that they have seen. Such a discussion will strengthen the knowledge of the students. As far as possible, the route for going and coming back should not be the same. If the students are brought back by a new route, it shall help them to acquire further knowledge.

After excursion, the calssroom teaching should be connected as far as possible with the things seen during excursion. A few days after excursion, only those things should be taught that have vital bearing on the places seen during the excursion.

If these precautions are taken and cosniderations are kept in mind while planning a historical excursion, the teaching of the history shall be made interesting, realistic and lasting.

Conclusions

1. Before 19th century, history was considered to be a dry and dull subject. With the advent of new thoughts in the

field of education, it was felt necessary to impart realistic touch to the teaching of history and so the provision of excursion war made.

2. Excursion may be arranged to the following places:

   (a) Old forts, battle places, historical places etc.

   (b) Historical museums and collection of historical coins, dresses, utensils, arms etc.

   (c) Places of historical significance, such as Agra, Fatehpur Sikri etc.

   (d) Places where excavation have been carried out, such as Mohanjodarao, Harappa etc.

   (e) Places where historical things like tombs, cave etc. exist.

   (f) Places of historical importance.

3. Excursions bring about the following advantages:

   (a) They make the classroom teaching interesting.

   (b) Develop love for cultural heritage.

   (c) Develop sentiments of partriotism in the students.

   (d) Help the students to acquire the knowledge of local history.

   (e) Bring about the development of different mental faculties.

4. While planning historical excursion, the following precautions and considerations should be borne in mind:

   (a) The teacher should know everything about the places of excursion.

   (b) The object of excursion should be determined with the help of the students.

(c) The students should be told about the things that they have to carry.

(d) The students should be divided into different groups so that they may understand things properly.

(e) They should be asked to make notes while on excursion.

(f) The teacher should explain the details about the places seen.

(g) Classroom teaching should also be connected with the excursion.

TECHNIQUES OF HISTORY TEACHING

Techniques of teaching should serve the ends and objectives of the society. India is a democratic country and so, the teaching of history should be conducted on the democratic lines. Prof. M. P. Muffut has very correctly laid down this fact in the following lines:

> "All techniques should be in line with democratic process and relate to the goods desired in the study of a topic. Techniques are employed for getting the learning underway with guidance from the teacher. They should be slected as a means of srving the best purpose of a particular time with the result of growth for the individual."

Various Techniques of Teaching History

Various techniques are employed in the teaching of history. These techniques are nothing but the ways of achieving the objectives of the teaching of history. Their aim is to make the knowledge intelligible, effective and useful. These techniques are of the following types:

1. Narration Technique
2. Drill Technique

3. Examination Technique
4. Question-answer Technique
5. Illustration Technique
6. Dramatization Technique

1. Narration Technique. In this technique, the teacher narrates the topic aand the students try to acquire knowledge through the narration. This narration is made with an eye on the interest, objectives and attitudes to the children. Attempt is made to way. Sometimes this technique is used as a supplementary for question-answer method.

Caution. While applying the technique of narration, the teacher should bear the following things in mind.

(a) The narration should be in accordance with the mental equipment and physical age of the children. The language should be such that it may ɔe understandable to the students of this age.

(b) The narration should not be very lengthy. The lengthy narrration is likely to spoil the intrest of the students.

(c) The narration, the teacher should also use of Question-answer method as a supplement to the technique. He should also use the teaching aids.

2. Drill Technique. This technique was originally introduced by Thorndike.This is, in fact, nothing but another form of the 'Trail and Error method.' This technique is based on the assumption that if a particular learning is revised several times, it becomes stable and permanent. Recapitulation makes the knowledge thorough and complete.

Limitations. This technique can be employed only in certain aspects of teaching of history. It is useful for learning the dates and names of the events.

Caution. While employing this method, the teacher should use it cautiously. It should be discreetly used for the purpose where it can be really useful.

3. Examination Technique. In this technique, the students are examined in regard to the knowledge of the subjects that they have learnt. Through this technique, it is ascertained how far the students have assimilated the subject taught.

The greatest advantage of this method is that it helps the teacher to ascertain how far he has been able to teach the lesson successfully.

Precautions. While using this method, the following precautions have to be observed:

(a) As far as possible, the test should be objective and the questions should be presented in a simple and intelligible language. The questions should be short and to the point.

(b) Attempt should be made to remove the difficulties of the students. In this regard, notes no answer books shall be useful.

(c) The teacher while marking, should be as impartial as he can do.

(d) The questions should cover the broadest possible field of learning.

4. Question-answer Technique. This is a very important technique in the teaching and study of history. Through questions, an attempt is made a ascertain and evaluate the knowledge of students in regard to the subject. Really speacking, in the modern education 'Question-answer technique' has acquired a very important place. This technique is employed to incite and awaken the curiosity in the students, and then through that curiosity, an attempt is made to improve their knowledge.

Merits. This is helpful in developing the power of expression of the students. This is also helpful in ascertaining their personal difficulties. On the basis of the knowledge acquired, an attempt may be made to remove the difficulties of the students.

Various Types of Questions. The real aim of the teachers should be the help the students to revise the subject-matter that they have been taught. Through these questions, their knowledge may also be tested.While framing questions, the teacher should keep in mind the mental age of the students. He should also try to see that these questions are pointed and meet the desired objective.

5. Illustration Technique. Through this technique, certain illustrations are presented before the students in order to make the subject material interesting and intelligible. In the modern set-up of education, a good deal of stress is laid on illustrations and examples.

Precautions. The illustrations and examples should be scientific and should have a direct bearning on the content material.

Types of Illustrations. These illustrations may be of various types, *viz.*, maps, sketches, models, charts, graphs, etc.

6. Drama Technique. In this technique of teaching history, an attempt is made to present the various events in a dramatic form. The students are asked to act scenes of certain periods of history by dialogues and by wearing the uniform.

In this technique, various sense organs of the students are kept active and busy. This leads to the development of a creative element in the students and a coordination is also established between the head and the hand. Shyness of the students is removed. This technique is quite useful for the healthy growth of the personality of the students.

HISTORY AS SCIENCE

History is a science, 'no less and no more,' said Bury. If history means enquiry or search and science 'an organised body of knowledge', then Bury's statement is a correct description of history. According to Lord Action the study of history is critical and objective. It is, a science.

History is a science in the sense that it pursues its own techniques to establish and interpret facts. Like Physics, Chemistry or Natural Sciences History is also an empirical field of study employing many methods of enquiry such as observation, classification, framing hypotheses and analysing evidence before interpreting the facts. Through the historian uses scienctific techniques, experiment is impossible since history deals with events that have already happened and cannot be repeated.

ARGUMENTS AGAINST HISTORY AS A SCIENCE

1. A scientist concentrates his attention on extracting general truths. He is in a position to predict. A historian, on the other hand, is engrossed in the peculiarities of a particular events. As W.H. Walsh has observed historians are not prophets but "a study of the history of a country or a movement does put us in a better position to forecast its future."

2. The course of human history is influenced by uncertain events. Therefore it is impossible to anticipate the future and predict it with any amount of certainty.

3. The facts of history are very complicated and seldom repeat in the real sense of the term.

4. The underlying facts of history have wide scope. They are so varied that they can seldom be uniform.

5. Historical data are not available for observation and experimentation.

6. Historical data are the products of human thoughts and action which are constantly changing. They, therefore, cannot provide dependable data for the formulation of general principles and laws.

LIMITS OF HISTORY AS SCIENCE

In history conflicting, divergent and varying accounts of the same theme have been given by various writers. A striking instance is that of the 'Event of 1857'. It has been delineated and described as an Indian War of Independence, a 'Mutiny, Rebellion, a Revolt and a Sepoy War, etc. The reasons for such different accounts are:

1. Personal prejudices.
2. Group prejudices.
3. Religious beliefs.
4. Racial differences.
5. National differences.
6. Theories of historical interpretation such as:
   - (i) cyclic.
   - (ii) religious.
   - (iii) liberal.
   - (iv) Marxist.

Explaining the limitations of History as a Science J.E. Swain writes: "The historian does not have the direct experience of the phenomena which he tries to explain. Napoleon's Moscow expendition cannot be reproduced in a laboratory, as the determination of the physical properties of water may be. Humanity is made up of individuals, no two of whom are alike. Indeed every person is distinctly new—no one in the past even approximated him closely if his entire make-up is considered. Every human being has something unique in spirit, if not in body. In Goethe's words, "The best in man has no form." Professor James H. Robinson concludes "The historian, from a narrow scientific point of view, is a little higher than a man of letters and a good deal lower than as astronomer of a biologist."

HISTORY AS SOCIAL SCIENCE

History is not a physical science but it is certainly a social science.

1. In history we have a collection of data from different sources.
2. A variety of methods are used to collect the data.
3. Collected data is very carefully and systematically analysed, classified and sorted.
4. The universe is the laboratory of history. Its ingredients are obtained from various human beings.
5. Certain principles and theories are laid down on the basis of observation, analysis and comparative studies of events.

OBJECTIVITY IN HISTORY

In the first volume of 'History of Civilization' published in 1857. Buckle, an English historian said history is still miserably deficient, and presents that confused and anarchical appearance natural to a subject of which the laws are unknown and even the foundations unsettled."

Leopold Von Ranke, a German teacher, said that if there is a meaning in history it can be discovered by a patient and detailed examination of the facts by men trained in the use of objective methods to be objective it is necessary that only what the documents reveal should be presented. This type of thinking resulted is devising critical methods for sifting, testing, collating and evaluating documentary sources. Most vigorous standards were pleaded in judging the objectivity, impartiality and accuracy of historical works.

The methods of its enquiry *viz.,* discovering and verifying the truths, formulating the hypothesis, locating the evidences, etc. are the methods of science. However, the material with which history deals is not observable or concreate as in the case of exact and natural sciences. Moreover, history cannot remain at the level of 'knowing' only. The construction and reconstruction of the past are inevitable parts of history. In this aspect the study of history becomes the study of art.

Regarding evolution of history as a science an NCERT publication says, "The evolution of history as a science is not complete, as it has no yet given sufficient emphasis to the development of general laws and to the prediction of future happenings. Its discussion of the general laws which might emerge from the discerning of causal relationship between social happenings and its indications of possible future happenings is as yet causal rather than systematic. In fact, some of the modern sciencs, such as Sociology. International Relations, etc., which have their origin in history, have outgrown the parent science in this matter."

TEACHING OF INDIAN HISTORY

D.D. Kosambi writes, "At the very outset we are faced with what appears to be an insuperable difficulty. India has virtually no historical records worth the name. Chinese imperial annals, country records, the work of early historians like Saum-Chien, inscriptions on graves and oracle-bones enable the history of China to be traced with some certainly from about 1400 B.C. Rome and Greece offer less antiquity, but far better historical literature. Even the Egyptian, Babylonian, Assyrian, and Sumerian records have been read. In India there is only a vague popular tradition, with very little documentation above the level of myth and legend.We cannot reconstruct anything like a complete list of Kings. Sometimes whole dynasties have been foregotten. What little is left is so nebulous that virtually no dates can be determined for any Indian personality till the Muslim period. It is very difficult to say over how much territory a great king actually ruled. There are no court annals in existence, with a partial exception for Kashmir and Chhamba. Similarly for great names in Indian literature. The works survive, but the author's date is rarely known. With luck, it may be possible to determine roughly the century to which the writing belonged; often it can only be said that the writer exited. Sometimes even that is doubtful; many a work known by a particular author's name could not possibly have been written by any one person."

A.L. Basham has observed, "The early history of India resemble a jigsaw puzzle with many misssing pieces, some part of the picture are fairly clear, others may be reconstructed with the aid of controlled imagination, but many gaps remain."

There is a dearth of historical writings in India. There are no historical treaties in the western sense. However, it is unfair to maintain that Indians had no sense of history. To quote A.C. Widgery, "Hindus have had and mostly still maintain definite attitudes to History to which expression is given in their philosophical and religious writings as in their practical religions and everyday life." C.H. Philips has remarked, "Historians of the people of the sub-continent have in the past operated rather like isolated guerilla, fighters in a jungle, often performing feats of individual brilliance, but lacking discipline and only vaguely aware of the part they should play in a general compaign.

FEATURES OF INDIAN HISTORY

1. Continuity. Jawahar Lal Nehru writes "that any culture of civilization should have this continuity for five of six thousand years or more, and not in a static, unchanging sense for India was changing and progressing all the time." R.C. Majumdar has observed, "Indian history and institutions form an unbroken chain by which the past is indissolubly linked with the present."

2. Unity. V.A. Smith writes "Unity that transcends the innumerable diversities of blood, colour, language, dress, manners and set." A.L. Basham thinks, "In the past, Hindu civilization has received, adapted and digested elements of many different cultures... we believe that Hindu civilization is in the act of performing its most spectacular feat of synthesis."

3. Variety. Jawahar Lal Nehru writes "She is like some ancient palimsest on which layer upon layer of thought and reverie had been inscribed and yet no succeedng layer had completely hidden or erased what had been written previously." The diversities of race, religion, caste and cultural development are the results of the continental size of the country, with its varied climate and vegetation and also of the numerous invasions of India since the dawn of history. India influenced them and was influenced by them.

4. Domination of Philosophy Over History. Metaphysical and moral trends of philosophy dominated the conception of history in ancient India. Very little attention was paid to the mere recording of facts and events. However, Jawahar Lal Nehru points out, "Lack of historical sense did not effect the masses; they built up their view of the past from traditional accounts, myths and stories...this imagined history, mixture of fact and legend gave an abiding cultural background. It is the living history built around historical events that had captured the imagination of the people and inspired their actions."

❑

6

Audio-Visual Aids

Audio-visual aids are the different types of useful materials, devices and symbols which make the study of a subject more comprehensible and interesting. Audio-visual aids are effective tools that "invest the past with an air of reality." They provide the learners with realistic experiences which capture their attentions and help in the understanding of the historical phenomena. They appeal to the mind through the visual aduditory senses and thereby enliven the past.They ensure a proper grasp of the subject and develop historical imagination.

The history teacher is under considrable pressure to make relevant what took place many centuries ago. He has to reconstruct a past which is shrouded in obscurity. Mere verbal descriptions cannot make history come alive, vivid and relevant to the lives of learners who are either present-oriented or future-oriented. A variety of teaching aids—pictures, maps, films, filmstrips, models, cartoons, time friezes and charts, graphs etc., can be drawn into the course, somewhat akin to raisins in the dough, and can be a welcome relief from normal routine. These aids can reinforce the teaching of history in many ways:

(1) Make History Real, Vivid, Vital, Interesting and Life-like. History is a subject which has gone into disrepute because of its dead uniformity and frozen and fixed account of facts. There is an urgent necessity of uplifting the teaching of history. The use of audio-visual aids can add zest, interest and vitality to any learning situations and make history a living subject.

(2) Help Pupils to Experience Historical Knowledge Directly. For example, we may not be able to witness now the route followed by Alexander for his invasion of India and the journey back, but we may see a map depicting the same. This is not time consuming. Also, it is a far better sources of knowledge than the verbal description of the route.

(3) Supplement the Spoken Word. History teaching inevitably deals with words which go beyond the experience of pupils. Use a vocabulary of politics, economics and the arts; talk of places not only in immediate vicinity but in different corners of the world; mention people not only of the immediate locality but of different times and climes. To make all these realistic and vivid before the pupils, mere chalking and talking will not help. The teacher must take the help of the audio-visual aids to supplement and explain the spoken word.

(4) Help in Developing a Sense of Time and Places. Use of time-line, for example, can help indicate how long ago did the Industrial Revolution take place; when England was passing through two golden periods of Elizabeth, India too was passing through the palmy days of Akbar. Similarly, use of a map will show the location of Delhi—how far is it from Deccan, how this distance was weakening the administration at the centre.

(5) Help the Teacher in Developing his Subject-matter. For example, a teacher may show pictures of Egyptian agriculture, metal workers at work, smelting and pouring the metal, and develop and lesson regarding occupations of the people by suitable questions.

(6) Develop Sense of Causal Relationship. History has to discuss the causal relations existing between happenings and has to trace the development of human society through such relationships.

(7) Supplement the Material of the Textbook. The audio and visual experience provided by these aids help in better understanding of the text. History rises above the history textbook.

(8) Help Making Learning Permanent. They say, history is a subject one forgets quickly. Through the utilisation of more than one sensory channel, the teacher of history can help to clarify, establish and correlate concepts, interpretations and appreciations. Thus, this will enable students to learn faster, remember longer, gain more accurate information and thus reinforce learning.

The use of audio-visual materials does not means a retreat from or abandonment of traditional reading, writing and speaking skills, but it does provide incentive to those students who have somehow not brought these aptitudes with them, even at the senior high level.

(9) Add Joy and Interest to Learning. Aid offer varied tyupes of experiences from direct, purposeful experiences to contrived experiences, dramatised experiences to demonstrations, field-trips, motion pictures, visual pictures, visual and verbal symbols. They thus, provide the students with a welcome 'break'. Students pay better attention in a class if they write, look, listen and read as they think. The aids add joy and interest.

It is rightly felt that students will best comprehend history if the ideas and concepts are defined and illustrated for them in a number of ways. It is the concentrated barrage of varied explanatory and illustrative materials requiring the exercise of different faculties and sense organs which finally penetrates the student's cortex. A teacher employing many tools in a complex and colourful presentation of his subject will find that he gets the material across to a far higher percentage of the students than if the were to instruct in simple, obvious routine ways.

ADVANTAGES OF AUDIO-VISUAL AIDS

1. Provision of Substitutes for Direct Experiences. It may not be possible for us to provide direct experience to our pupils while studying events from the past or from life in far-away lands. Audio-visual materials facilitate the understanding of new concepts, facts and symbols. Pictures, models and specimens etc., are used as accurate and effective substitutes of direct leanring experiences. The study of particular films and still pictures is more econmical.

2. Provision of Sensory Experience. These provide an adequate back-ground of senory experience essential for learning. New words and unfamiliar objects are attached to specific elements of one's experience. Both direct and indirect learning experiences are important in the teaching of History. As senses are the gateways of learning, lessons should have a multiple sense appeal. Things of audio-visual aids stimuli which appeal to more than one sense organ, are perceived and remembered easier and better.

3. Motivation. Audio-visual aids are very important motivators. They materials process vividness, clarity and dramatic appeal. As children enjoy looking at pitures, going to movies and listening to the radio, these can be an effective medium to hold attention and to stimulate new interests and activities among children. These can motivate pupils to learn faster, remember longer, gain more accurate information and better understand the delicate concept and meanings.

4. Supplement to Direct Experience. Audio-visual aids supplement direct experiences by vicarious or representative learning. The pupils may visit a post office or a cotton textile mill. If their direct learning experiences are followed by the study of a film or motion picture on the subject. They can learn still more about the postal system and about the manufacture of cloth. The such a film adds to the information already gained from actual visits and trips.

5. More Efficient Learning. By the proper use of audio-visual aids pupils learn more rapidly and also remember the facts, thus learned, for longer period. When a child sees, hears, touches, tastes and smells, his experiences are concrete, and more or less permanent. As the mental images created by pictures, models, charts and other such aids are easy to recall, more efficient memorisation is possible.

6. Aid for the Slow Learner. Audio-visual aids particularly helpful for poor readers and slow learners. Who do not get all the required knowledge from the text-book and stay backward. The can more easily understand and remember the facts, gained through pictures, movies, models and radio etc.

7. Development of the Power of Imagination and Observation. Image is the greates instrument of instruction. Audio-visual aids provide sensory images more clear and effective than the verbal images. Learning is made natural and easy. Audio-visual aids stimulate imagination and develop the power of observation, analysis and synthesis. Students ability to analyse, compare, generalize and synthesize rests upon the broad base of experience effectively supply by audio-visual aids.

8. Meaningful Learning. Verbal desriptions are often vague and unsatisfactory. Teachers often talk of abstract thins beyond the comprehesion of young children. But the meaningful material is learned and assimilated by the child very easily. It is forgotten at a slower speed. Larning involves not only knowledge but also meaning of things. Rich meaning means rich learning. The children are liable to forget those things which do not mean much for them. Audio-visual aids break the monotony of the formal type of teaching.

CONE OF EXPERIENCE

Edger Dale has classified the audio-visual aids on the basis of the kinds of experience presented through the aid. He calls it the 'Cone of Experience', which ranges from direct experience to pure abstraction. According to him these divisions are not rigid. "The cone device, then, is visual metaphor of learning experiences, in which the various types of audio-visual materials are arranged in the order of increasing abstractness as one proceeds from direct experiences."

Stages in Cone Device

1. The base of the cone represents direct reality—the rich, full-bodied experience that is the bed rock of all education.

2. The second, state in the development of increasingly abstract experience involves the use of contrivances like models—an 'editing' of reality.

3. The third stage is the reconstruction of experiences through dramatics. It steps in where contrived experiences fail.

These three cone bands involve action. "Thus, in the direct experience, obtained through such a contrivance as a working model or a mock-up and in the experience of reconstructing reality by acting in a dramatisation—in there these the students is not a spectator but a participant."

4. The next stage of abstraction from reality is reached when the student's participation goes on decreasing and he becomes a spectator. Demonstrations, field trips, exhibits, television, motion pictures, radio, recordings and pictures, come under this category. In these we simply watch and listen. These aids provide realistic reproduction of the things.
5. The final stage leads to verbal symbols—"designations that hear no physical resemblance to the objects or ideas for which they stand." They simply signify that a certain word stands for an object, an idea, a scientific principles, or a philosophical aphorism.
6. Higher up in this cone of experience are the visiul symbols, like charts, graphs, maps and diagrams which are simply an abstract representation of the reality.

CLASSIFICATION OF AUDIO-VISUAL AIDS

(1) Visual Aids

(i) Chalk Board and Bulletin Board

(ii) Charts

(iii) Pictures

(iv) Graphs

(v) Maps and Globes

(vi) Stereoscopes

(vii) Motion Pictures (Silent)

(viii) Objects, Specimens and Models

(2) Auditory Aids

(i) Radio

(ii) Dictaphone

(iii) Loud speaker

(iv) Phonograph

(v) Gramophone

(3) Audio-visual Aids

(i) Television

(ii) Sound Motion Pictures

(iii) Dramatisation

(iv) Field Trips and School Journeys.

Excursions and Field Trips

Excursions and field-trips can provide unparalled learning experiences particularly in the teaching of history. They can provide first hand observation and new infromation to enable the students to realise that history is not merely a story. They can add spice and break the monotony of history lessons. They are of great use for developing an appreciation of architecture, sculpture, painting, etc. They are helpful in illustrating the historical method, a they are, in fact, the source of history. With their help attempts can be made in cooperation with the pupils to build up history of any particular historical happening.

Kinds of Trips. Trips can be of various kinds:

1. Trips within the school or trips within a walking distance.
2. Longer trips in the community to historic spots.
3. Trips in vacations for a week or so to Delhi, Bombay, Calcutta, Ajanta or Ellora caves or other special places of interest.
4. Day trips to a state capital, college, historic spot, etc.

Criteria for Selecting Trips. The following criteria may be useful for selecting trips:

1. It should provide something that can be learnt better by direct experience than by textbooks, films and other methods.
2. A trip should be related to the topic under discussion, as a follow-up on the topics studied, or as motivation for a new topic.
3. It should give students experience that they cannot easily have alone, in small groups or with parents.
4. It must have the approval of parents and school adminstration.
5. The distance should not be too long for the time available.
6. The expenses should be low.

Preparation, Conduct and Follow-up. Excursions and trips can prove useful if they are well planned, well conducted and well followed-up. For this purpose, a number of hints are suggested below:

1. The teacher should make a survey of the local possibilities in regard to original material in history. He should then work out a plan for historical trips and excursions for a whole session, closely correlating such plans with teaching of history in the class.
2. The pupils should be carefully prepared for the trip or excursion. They should have an idea of what to expect and how the new information will be useful. Merely looking at some objects may not be educative. Thorough preparation should be made with the help of appropriate questions, references, reports, stories, clippings, pictures, motion pictures, etc.

3. Every detail of the trip should be carefully and completely worked out beforehand. Nothing should be left to chance. Once the plans are made they should be followed as closely as possible.

4. Each trip should be carefully evaluated, the record of which may be kept for future guidance.

5. The trips should be carefully followed up also. A variety of activities including diaries, photos, bulletin boards, articles in the school magazine, thank you-letters, etc., cap help in the follow-up. Discussion of various features at appropriate time can also be of help.

6. The trip should be carefully supervised so that it is really a serious educational opportunity, not a gay picnic.

7. After the return, the experiences from the trip should be systematised and correlated to the history lesson.

Possibilities of Excursion and Trips in the Community. Every comunity offers innumerable possibilities and opportunites for excursions and trips. No teaching possibility in the area should be overlooked. The only point which is to be borne in mind is that the excursion must suit the age level of the pupils. Following are some of the possibilities of direct study of historical materials.

(i) Monuments, battlefields, sties of historical events, old forts, etc.

(ii) Tombs, memorials, burial grounds, etc.

(iii) Places of worship, temples, mosques, etc.

(iv) Museums and old houses with relics of historical interest such as weapons, utensils, costumes, paintings, culture, old manuscripts, etc.

(v) Administrative and legislative centres with records of historical decisions and happenings.

(vi) Sites of excavations, etc.

(vii) Art galleries.

(viii) Ruins of capitals and educational centres.

Models

Original materials are quite rare in history. Even those which exist are within easy reach of all schools. Therefore, the models—the three dimensional representations of real things—can be used with great advantages in the teaching of history.

A model may be defined as a replica of an object as it is or in a reduced or in an enlarged form. Models can afford a sustitute for most of the historic remains. They give a vivid impression of the real.

Use of models in teaching helps in visualising the historical reality such as buildings, sculptures, etc. Sometimes, models may be the shortest and easiest way of presenting certain concepts to pupils. For explaining the peculiarities of Gandhara sculpture, observing a single work of the age may be far more educative than verbal description of the type of sculpture.

Models can invest history with the sense of reality. Things which were mere stories to the pupils might appear as true if we have models to support our verbal exposition.

Types of Models. A variety of models can be used for illustrating history.

(i) Models of personalities who have made their contributions to history in specific fields—political, religious, social and economic and cultural. Such models help pupils to identify themselves with personalities and, thus, every event connected with them becomes more meaningful and interesting. Models of personalities are useful in the junior classes.

(ii) Models of armours and weapons of different ages directly convey historical information. They can be used for class dramatisation and exhibitions, besides ordinary day-to-day lessons.

(iii) Models of pillars and rock inscriptions add to the effectiveness of history lessons.

(iv) Models of places which are sites of events of the greatest historical importance, for example, Kurukshetra and the battlefields of Panipat, and Plassey can develop pupils' interest in the study of history. They can also be used in exhibitions.

(v) Models of human dwellings, utensils, ornaments, custumes, etc., in different ages are very useful in history teaching. They may also be used for class dramatisations and exhibitions, besides ordinary history teaching.

(vi) Models illustrating agriculture, means of transport, and communication through the ages, can create an interest in the proces of development and impress upon the students the extent of man's progress.

(vii) Models of documents or copper plates (in clay or plaster of paris) can go a long way in teaching history by the source method.

(viii) Models of architecture and sculpture are very useful in development proper concepts. Such models are available from commercial firms.

(ix) Models of gods and goddesses worshipped during the different ages can help in creating proper awareness among pupils regarding the process of religious development.

AUDIO-VISUAL PICTURES

With tremendous development in the field of science and technology, with the help of projectors, the teacher can create the third dimension illusion, sustain the interest of the pupils in the topic and enable them to understand the past happenings in their true setting, though following audio-visual pictures:

1. Still Pictures. Still pictures are projected with the help of opaque projectors, standard lanterns, overhead slide lanterns, film strip projectors or other devices to help the pupils to have an idea of past realities. The opaque projector can project photographs, cards, cartoons, coins, paper, money, maps, drawings and the like. Standard lantern projects materials reproduced on glass slides. Slide Lantern projects pictures and facilitates discussion by the teacher while the picture is in progress. The film strip projector projects pictures printed on a strip of film instead of on a glass slide.

2. Motion Pictures. Appyling a more advanced technique than discussed above, Motion Pictures introduce an element of motion in the contents and thereby impart continuity in the theme. Along with sound, they bring an element of realism in the classroom. They represent historical events in their proper perspective, showing their causal sequence and continuity. The pupils transcend the limitations of time and plae and become live in the midst of historical events. Historical facts and events are remembered easily. The emotional impact of such films is enormous.

3. Films-Kinds

(i) ***Classroom Films.*** There are made for use inside the classroom for showing the development of the important political, social and economic movements, for dramatising the life of great men and women, etc.

(ii) ***Documentary Films.*** These present the story of the historical events as they do happen.

(iii) ***News Reels.*** These also represent historical phenomena.

(iv) Photoplays are means to depict the life of some great personalities or dramatise some historical happenings. Tinged with imagination, photo plays give realistic picture about the principal event, and its social and geographical setting.

Advantages

Films have tremendous educational potentialities as the most powerful instrument of communication. Thomas A. Edison once declared, "The only text-book needed will be for the teacher's own use. Films will serve as guide post to these teacher-instruction books, not the books as guide to the films. Pupils will learn from films everything there is in every grade from the lowest to the highest... Films are inevitable to become practically the sole teaching method." Through the films are not going to replace the teacher in near future but as an aid to teaching they play a dominant role. "We may not be able to accompany Tenzing Norkay to climb the Himalayas or visit the Pyramids in Egypt but through motion pitures we can 'visit' as well as 'accompany'. Not all of us can go to U.K. or U.S.A. or have an expedition to the Poles or look into a microscope that shows the blood cells but we can see all these through the motion pictures vividly and clearly."

4. Film Strips or Film Slides. A useful means of teaching history effectively. Film strips are made up of 20 to 100 or more individual pictures printed on a roll of film of 35 mm. width. Verbal explanations of the pictures and sometimes continuity are provided by *(1)* titles which are superimposed on the pictures or printed on separate *(2)* an accompanying guide in a pamphlet form, *(3)* a recorded lecture.

Easy and simple to use, the film strips, are light in weight and can be efficiently used to produce bright pictures in a room partially lighted. Relatively inexpensive too every school can easily provide for them. The class can examine the pictures on the screen as long as desirable.

Graphs

Graphs are flat pictures which employ dots, lines or pictures to visualies numerical and statistical data to show statistics or relationships. They are made according to exact satisfications and depict specifically quantitative data for analysis, interpretation or comparison.

Graphs are effective tools for making comparisons and contrasts. The use of visual imageries for abstract ideas helps clarification and remembrance.

Kinds of Graphs. *(1)* Line graph, *(2)* Bar graph, *(3)* Circle graph, *(4)* Pictorial graph.

In history teaching, the Line graph and the Bar graph can prove very useful.

Line Graph. The line graph is used when there are a considerable number of data to be plotted or when the data are continuous. The concepts are represented with the help of simple lines, vertically or horizontally drawn. Variations of the line graph include the high, low, and shaded line graph. Pictorial illustrations and cartoons are occasionally used on line graphs to increase their interest and readability. A shaded line graph attacts more than a solid line graph because it provides more contrast.

Bar Graph. Here inter-related satistical information is presented by means of bars vertically or horizontally made.

Pictorial Graph. Pictorial graph is an outstanding method of graphic representation. Pictures are used for the expression of ideas. They are thus more attractive and are easily understood. In a pictorial graph, a complete story is told with pictures. The number of size of the pictures conveys the proportionate amount. It is not as exact as other types of graphs, because there is a certain amount of estimation on quantity. Children like them, and they are useful with adults. Graphs, being symbolic and abstract in character, are best used in the body and summary of a lesson after the student has acquired a background of information from other sources.

GRAPHS

Graphs are utilised to represent quantitative data showing comparison, trends, developments and relationships. With the help of simple lines, drawn vertically or horizontally, graphs supply visual imageries for abstract ideas and concepts in history.

1. Time Line. Time line gives linear representation of time. It helps the pupils to gain time sense with the help of space symbols. In a time line, the length of time is symbolically represented by a line drawn horizontally or vertically. It gives a visual image of the sequence of events and their relative differences in their occurrence in time. It helps us in comparing and contrasting relationship between events and happening at different places at the same time.

The pupils should understand the symbolic meaning of the time line. The history teacher should classify the concept. The units of the time line should be equal in length. Dates should be located in the time line whenever he makes reference to such dates.

2. Pictorial Graph. It expresses an idea or a concept with the help of picture symbols which are self-explanatory and appropriate. The symbols usually used are man, ship, horse, elephants, money, etc. Their total qualities are shown by proper number or multiple of the symbols. The numerical value of each unit is shown by a key.

3. Histogram. It represents an idea with the help of broad lines or narrow rectangles, drawn vertically or horizontally. The scale of values is placed at the bottom in horizontal and at the left in a vertial arrangement. The broad lines or rectangles may be coloured or differentiated in some other ways. Histograms may be utilised to represent growth and fall of empires or some other historical phenomena.

Summits at a Glance

Summit	*Venue*	*Dates and Years*	*Membership*
1	*2*	*3*	*4*
First	Belgrade	September 1-6, 1961	28 countries
Second	Cairo	October 5-10, 1964	47 countries 10 observers
Third	Lusaka	September 6-10, 1970	54 countries 11 observers 7 guests

1	*2*	*3*	*4*
Fourth	Algiers	September 5-9, 1973	75 countries 24 observers 7 guests
Fifth	Colombo	August 16-19, 1976	86 countries 22 observers 18 guests
Sixth	Havana	September 3-9, 1979	94 countries 20 observers 7 guests
Seventh	New Delhi	March 7-11, 1983	96 countries 26 observers and guests

DIAGRAMS

Diagrams represent historical facts and events with the help of visual symbols which convey a number of things within a short space and time. They help to present historical data in an interesting way and captivate of the pupils attention. The history teacher should see that diagrams are constructed with care and caution. They should be technically correct. They should use symbols which are handy and easy to draw. They should appropriate talks. Artistically presented they should appeal to the aesthetic sense of the pupils. Many themes such as, sources of history, important battles, administrative systems, comparison and contrast between religions, life in early civilisation may be diagramatically presented.

Charts may be defined as combinations of graphic and pictorial media designed for the orderly and logical visualising of relationship between key facts and ideas. The main function of the charts is always to show relationships such as comparisons, relative amounts, developments, processes, classification and rganisation.

Types of Charts. There are many types of charts:

1. Genealogy charts
2. Flow charts
3. Relationship charts
4. Tabulation charts
5. Chronology charts

Most commonly used charts in history are genealogy charts, flow charts, chronology charts and tabulation charts.

Genealogy Charts. Genealogy Charts are used to represent the growth and development of an empire or dynasty. Taking an analogy from the tree, the origin is a single line, rectangle, circle or other representations of the trunk and the various changes or developments are shown as the branches. Such charts have been traditionally used in history to represent blood relationships between the members of the same line with the help of visual symbols.

Flow Charts. Flow Charts are used to show sequence and the functional relationship as the organisation of city administration, the relationship between the executive, judicial and legislative departments or the relationship of different rulers, United Nation's Structure etc. This is done when there is continuity and a chain of historical events and sequence. In this chart, lines, rectangles, circles or other graphic representation are connected by lines showing the directional flow of the organisation. While designing a flow chart, care must be taken to preserve a sense of order and sequence.

Chronology Charts. Chronology Charts provide a chronological framework within which events and developments may be recorded. They develop a times sense among the pupils, helping them to comprehend and visualise the pageant of time and its relationship. The relation between the different aspects for example, political developments, cultural achievements, religious changes, foreign relations, etc., can be most easily shown in a chronology chart. The preparation of a chronology chart can be a class activity, a group activity or an individual piece of work. It can be planned to last one year, three years or even through the five years of a secondary school.

In constructing chronology charts, the following hints can prove useful:

(a) Only important dates should be inserted.

(b) They should represent only space relations.

(c) The scale used should be accurate and uniform.

(d) They should be beautifully built so as to capture the imagination and attention of the pupils and have a picturesque effect. Different types of symbols might be used in order to distinguish the various features.

Tabulation Chart. Here the historical data is presented in a tabular form. It enables us to gain a comprehensive view of the facts at sight. The data is analysed under several heads and sub-heads. Themes such as great battles of Indian history may be analysed under the heads—name of the battle, year in which fought, the parties involved, the results and significance etc.

MAPS AND GLOBES

Maps are the universally accepted symbols representing historical reality in space. They show the location, distance and direction of places connected with historical events. They give information about the distribution of land, water, vegetable life, climate, economic resources which have directly or indirectly shaped the destiny of man. Maps help to visualise historical realities supplementing their oral and written account.

Globe gives a three dimension representation of the earth and may be conveniently used in showing historical events like World Wars I and II and other events of universal character.

(i) Relief Maps. There are useful in showing the depressions and elevations on the surface of earth which have influenced the course of history. Invasions, military operations, migration of the people and social intercourse, all bear the impact of the inequalities in the surface of the earth.

(ii) Layer Charts. These give a clear picture of historical phenomena.

(iii) Flat Maps. Showing physical features, political divisions, population, rainfall, temperature, soil, vegetation, menas of transport and communication of the world and other countries. These provide ample oppotunites for illustrating history lessons.

The teacher should encourage the pupils to draw maps. It will given them joy and at the same time add to their knowledge places related with history. They should draw simple maps in the beginning and complicated maps when they have learnt the art of using lines, symbols, colours, etc. effectively.

DRAMATISATION

Dramatisation helps the history teacher to make the past real. History is concerned not only with places and objects but also with events, ideas and institutions wieh have been preserved through verbal symbols. It does not proceed through isolated phenomenon. It has a causal sequences, one event leads to another event and the process continues. Human intentions, designs and motives behind every event cannot be presented through visual symbols. They can be made real dramatisation.

Dramatisation is an attempt to act or to do as others have acted or done. It is the depition of characters, movements, and activities of a story or a play through facial expression, gesture and bodily actions accompanied by the use of language. With its conerete appeal to the sense of sight as well as to the sense of hearing dramatisation makes an ardent appeal to the children. "It attempts to tell the story in more vivid manner than by word alone, and to enrich the appeal of the play through the addition of the pictorial element found in the movement of speaking characters across the stage."

Advantages

1. Full of education potentialities, Dramatisation presents an emotional situation necessary for effective learning. It provides an outlet for the discharge of extra energy of the pupils and thereby gives them poise and balance of mind.

2. In history dramatisation reconstrus past experiences of historical significance. It provides opportunity for vivid realistic and full representation of a happening or a situation in history.

3. It transcends the barrier of time and place and relives the experience concerned. Through the use of language, accompanied by bodily actions and supported by proper setting, it helps bring out the customs, the language, and the mannerisms of the period.

4. In dramatisation, the pupils who play the role of different character of history, feel like those characters and become the characters to a degree. K.P. Choudhury says, "The pupils assimilate the essential facts by playing the different historical characters and by reconstructing the important historical events, in the connection. Those who dose not directly participate in dramatisation but witness it, also get in the spirit and in case of successful acting they are also carried away with the characters—the experience becoming almost as real to them as to the actors".

5. Dramatisation provides an excellent opportunity for group work and social participation and many practical works in history can be correlated with it.

6. Dramatisation is an effective method of providing an opportunity fortearning by doing in history.

Kinds of Dramatisation

1. Full Length Plays. These provide an opportunity for the vivid, realistic and full representation of an idea, happening or a situation in history. They require detailed preparation, careful rehearsals, proper costumes and well-arranged stage setting.

(i) ***Themes.*** Themes like the story of Ramayana, the story of Mahabharata, the life of Buddha, Alexander and Porus. Chandra Gupta and Seleukos, the life of Harshvradhana, Akbar and Rana Partap. Shivaji and Aurangzeb from Indian history, may be taken for dramatisation. Ever such events may be dramatised accroding to the age and educational standards of the pupils. Historical plays written by experts or prepared by the cooperation of the history teacher and pupils, staged as the joint project of the pupils of all ages and of all abilities, may be staged on social functions in connection with important school days.

(ii) ***Staging.*** Not more than three or four plays during the session may be successfully staged as such plays require great preparation. The histroy teacher may arrange less formal dramatisation with the help of his class once in a month. The theme of such dramas should be important events and characters in the history course of the class. The pupils should be initiated in undertaking reading for the play, writing out dialogues, preparing stage materials and make-ups and so on. The play may be staged during school hours or on one of the saturdays or on some other occasions.

(iii) ***Plays in Classroom.*** The history teacher may undertaken even less formal dramatisation. He may prepare the pupils for the lesson through different devices and then proceed on formal teaching. Historical events or happenings may be presented to the pupils by asking them to play the role of the different historical characters. The application of the knowledge gained or recapitulation of the lesson, may be done with the help of dramatisation.

2. The Pageant. Another from of dramatisation Pageant is helpful in depicting an idea or a feeling by arranging a spectacle. The great emperors, social and religious reformers in India may appear in a line each with his distinctive dress. Indian art through the ages, the best works from architecture, sculpture and painting may also be presented through pageants.

3. The Pantomine. Pantomine is a play in which the participants express themselves through bodily actions, usually to the acompaniment of music. It provides opportunity to learn to be communicative with facial expression and bodily gestures. It gives shy children a release from their inhibitions. In history action without words is by far the most telling mode of communication in many situations.

4. Puppetry. One of the most significant forms of dramatisation Puppetry from human drama. Its appeal is universal. Its characters have their own personality and are not swayed by human emotions. It provides a natural charm and leave enough scope for imagination. It presents ideas with extreme simplicity yet effectively without elaborate scenery or costume. Themes like India on the Day of the Independence, a Session of the Congress, and Round Table Conference, may be effective presented through puppet shows.

5. The Tableau. Tableau is more effective device for representing emotional theme. It is a picture-like scene of human characters, presented against the background of their action. For example Budha may be shown as appearing like a light agent the back ground of misery. Ashoka may be shown to be receiving a new inspiration in the battle field of Kalinga.

Considerations in Staging Historical Plays:

1. Work as a guide, the teacher should not try to dominate the show. While initiative should come from the pupils the teacher should direct them from the back ground.

2. Depending on the events chosen for dramatisation and time at the disposal of the teacher and the pupils. The play may

be prepared by the teachers with the cooperation of the pupils. We may select plays written by great writers. Plays so chosen must illuminate the most significant periods in the political, social, economic and religious development of a people.

3. The stage requirements, such as stage settings and scenery should be as far as possible within the reach of the pupils.
4. Characters should be chosen in such a way that every pupil gets an opportunity to take part in some activities and some pupils do not monopolise all the activities.
5. Dramatisation should be followed by discussions on the different aspects of the events or happenings.

PUPPETRY

Puppetry is a specialised form of dramatisation which ordinarily employs doll-like figures of human or animal forms. The puppets may be mechanically operated or by hand with the help of strings. It is the operator who speaks for the puppet in different tones and plays several roles.

Puppetry has two main forms: *puppets and marionettes.* Puppets which are simpler to make and operate, are held and moved by the hands of the operator. Marionettes are manipulated by strings, wires or rods from a different level.

If the teacher knows the operation of puppets, he may deliver a whole lesson in history through the puppets. There can also be puppet shows with proper use of light and stages effects.

Puppetry has got certain distinctive advantages. It can present ideas with extreme simplicity without elaborate scenery and costumes, yet quite effectively. Distracting details are eliminated so that attention is focussed on the dramatised experience itself.

After every puppet show, there should be follow-up work in the class. Puppet shows have the greatest appeal for pupils of primary classes, but can be used with profit with pupils of higher classes also.

Suggestive list of events for full-length plays

1. Alexander and Porus
2. Shivaji and Aurangzeb
3. Prithviraj and Sanyogita
4. Akbar and his nine jewels
5. Guru Nanak and his teachings
6. Chandragupta and Chanakya
7. Harishchandra
8. Jesus Christ and his teaching, etc.
9. Buddha and his teachings

Suggestive list of events for class dramatisation

1. Ashoka's propagation of the Dhamma
2. Buddhism—its spread
3. Golden Age of the Guptas—A scene in the court of Chandragupta and Vikramaditya could be damatised
4. Round Table Conference
5. A Congress session
6. Sher Shah's administrative system

Important points for successful historionics

(i) In introducing histrionics in class-rooms, we should carefully see that the class takes them seriously.

(ii) The teacher should not dominate the shows; he should only direct and guide from the background. Pupils should be encouraged to come forward and express themselves.

(iii) There is no need for stage setting and scenery in a classroom play. The chalk-board can present forests and a cleared space can become a market place. The emphasis should be on action, gesturs, expression, voice and interpretation rather than on clothes, scenery and setting.

(iv) Histrionics must be properly followed up. Questions, wisely chosen by the teacher, should open up wide discussions and ultimately help in increasing knowledge and understanding.

(v) Characters should be chosen as appropriately as possible. Teacher should take care that some pupils do not monopolise all the activities.

PICTURES

Children, by their very nature, are picture-minded. This love of pictures can be capitalised to add zest, interest and vitiality to the teaching of history.

Pictures, they say, concretise history—they help children to understand that history is concerned with real things, real places and real persons. They are representations of beautiful dreams of reality or at least beautiful dreams. "If history is to be made interesting, particularly for lower classes, the proper materials for teaching are dramatic scenes and heroic characters." Abstract generalisations—are always cumbersome. Pictures will simplify the abstractions and help create and maintain interest.

Types of Pictures

(a) Pictures made on Charts or Pasted on Charts. These can prove very useful for teaching. Pictures of great reformers, personages, kings, battlefields, scenes from the courts, architecture, costumes, armours, life in primitive times and afterwards, development of means of transport, development of war weapons, development of postal system etc., are very useful in teaching history.

(b) Picture post-cards. Picture post-cards showing historical sites and buildings, museums and monuments, art galleries and courts etc., are very useful.

(c) Textbook and Reference Pictures. They help and supplement the reading material in history.

(d) Pageant-type Aids. For the primary classes well drawn and coloured portraits are very useful as the children at this stage are interested in personalities and their activities. If a number of portraits are presented in a chronological order, they may help in covering the presentation of a selected number of historical topics. For example, the Bhakti Movement may be presented with the help of pictures of the various saints. Similarly, topics like social reformers, leaders in the struggle for independence can also be illustrated through pageant-type aids. Pageant-type presentations can also be used for teaching topics like postal system, agricultural implements, domestic, utensils in India, houses, war weapons through the ages, dresses of the people in different states of India, stone agee culture, etc.

(e) Picture-assembly. This is another useful device for making history intersting and effective. It has been seen that a single picture cannot present a historical topic; a number of pictures can be assembled together to present it. For example, a topic like Shah Jahan as a builder may be presented with the help of following pictures; a portrait of Shah Jahan in the centre and pictures of his typical buildings around the portrait with suitable captions. Topics like social reforms in India after 1858, religious reforms in India after 1858, nationalist movement from 1905-1918, Roman civilization at a glance, reformation in Europe, democratic and nationalist movements after 1815, etc., can be presented through picture-assembly. Old illustrated journals and calendars are rich sources for collecting historical pictures. Photographs are also available in all historical places. These pictures may be assembled aesthtically according to the requirements.

(f) Picture-Diagram. This is another popular device used to present concepts in history in visual form, parrticularly with senior students. Here, pictures, instead of words, are used to present abstract concepts, whereas in pageant and picture-assumbly types of presentation, concrete objects or actual hapenings are presented in pictures; in pictured diagrams, abstract ideas are presented in picture-symbols, the objects drawn or painted are mere symbols, they represent other ideas that are apparently presented by the pictures. The ideas represented are also indicated by appropriate titles.

(g) Cartoon. A cartoon does not present the reality directly; it is a mataphorical presentation of reality. The cartoonist depends on humour, satire and mockery for the presentation of his idea. In a way, the cartoon is also a picture-diagram, as it presents ideas rather than real objects. Cartoon-type presentation makes a strong appeal to the emotions, thus it enhances learning. This device should be used with pupils of higher classes as a higher level of intellectual maturity is required to appreciate the idea behind a cartoon.

Sources of Pictures. There are many sources from which pictures can be obtained easily and inexpensively. Some of these are—newspapers, especially Sunday supplements, magazines like *Life, Time, Chandamama, Nandan, Pictorial Reviews, Illustrated Weekly of India* etc. The teacher should encourage the pupils in the collection of appropriate pictures.

Qualities of Pictures. Pictures are supposed to supplement the spoken word. It is essential that they should be of the highest quality. They should be purposeful, relevant, significant, truthful, authentic, up-to-date complete, simple, stimulative, suggestive of reality and interesting. They should be large enough to the easily seen and understood by the pupils sitting on the last bench. The pictures should be free from smudges, blurs, scratches or blemishes and have good captions or apt descriptions.

Using Pictures Effectively. Selecting a good picture and preparing it for class-work is useless unless the picture is utilised effectively. Below are given some suggestions for effective use of pictures:

(i) The pupils must be led to look into the pictures. They must be guided to see actively, critically, and personal satisfaction.

(ii) A picture leaves much to the imagination. Some of the things such as distance, speed, action, height, weight, breadth, sound, etc., are mere distractions. Just exposing the picture will not help to convey all these ideas. For proper interpretation and understanding, a picture must be taught intelligently and explained clearly.

(iii) Sufficient time should be given to comprehend a pciture. Learning should not be handicapped by hustle and hurry, which brings inadequate and careless response and often unpreared and untimely anticipation of the next point. The pupils must learn not only to look at pictures but to look into them, understand the details and interpret them.

(iv) Pictures should be closely related to the lesson, as unrelated pictures serve only to distract attention.

(v) Small pictures should be used for individual or group study.

(vi) Too many pictures should not be shown in one lesson. Studying a few carefully selected pictures is more profitable than merely looking at a greater number.

(vii) Loose pictures can be displayed on the bulletin board with notes or question attached which direct or challenge the children's observations.

TELEVISION

A more advanced instrument than the radio Television makes an appeal to both the visual and auditory sense. It is "medium of mass communication which far surpasses in effectiveness anything our civilization has yet known." It is commonly said that the television is "the black board dramatised, the picture brought to life." It accomplishes certain communicative tasks incomparable in their effectiveness. It incorporates some of the distinctive contributions of other audio-visual materials—demonstrations, chalk broad, chart, model etc.

With its two-fold engagment of the eye and the motion pictures, Television can bring us into contact with events in an exciting and clarifying way. It is a "means by which teachers, parents, children, and all citizens may share a common experience at the same time."

A versatile vehicle to use a beauty of audio-visual materials, it introduces vitality and novelty which attracts attention, creates interest and stimulates learning.

It transports the places and sites of historical importance which the pupils are unable to visit. It brings the experts in the classroom not only in voice but in person. It makes available to the classroom rare examples of natural or man-made objects.

In India, facilities for teaching through television are available in the schools of Delhi only. In the near future, it is hoped that it will push back radios and make the teaching of history vivid, real and interesting.

PHONEGRAPH RECORDS

Phonegraph records are auditory devices utilised to make an appeal to auditory sense and invest the past with a sense of reality. Easily he adapted to teaching. These records can be used at the psychological moment when it is most needed and when it will be most effective in the lesson. Played more than once record can be used very effectively in the teaching of subjects, like history.

Slides

Slides are becoming increasingly popular in history teaching. They are relatively inexpensive to purchase, can be quite easily constructed and stored, and may be used countless times without deterioration. They possess an attention focusing power which increases class interest and motivation. They can be projected in a partially darkened room thus facilitating the class discussion and note taking. They can be enlarged to any desired size, repeatedly shown and held on the screen for any period of time. They are quite flexible in that a variety of printed typed or drawn materials can be presented in many different colours or combinations.

Careful planning is necessary to make the most efficient use of slides. The slides can be used to introduce the lesson. They can be used during the development of the lesson and also for summarising the lesson. They can even be used for evaluation. It is necessary that slides are worked into the lesson-plan.

A few examples are given below to explain the point:

(1) The teacher can prepare the students for a lesson on Indus Valley Civilisation by projecting the slides of Mohenjodaro and Harappa.

(2) A lesson on Shivaji may be introduced by showing a few pictures of Maharashtra.

(3) Lesson on Mauryan Art, Gupta Art, Mughal Art and the like could very effectively be presented through pictures.

(4) Life of Buddha can be presented to the class with the help of a few slides.

(5) Shahjahan's buildings could very well be presented with the help of slides.

(6) Guru Nanak's travel may be presented by a few pictures of the route he took and the places he visited.

Slide albums are available on social sciences which could go a long way in making the lessons lively and interesting.

The effective use of slide necessitatives the following:

(1) The teacher should know how to operate the projector with ease and confidence.

(2) The teacher is fully conversant with the contents of slides and their educational potentialities.

1. Chalk-Board. The chalk-board is one of the most valuable aids for making instruction in history concrete and understandable. When it is used properly, it can set standards in neatness, accuracy and speed. An illustration drawn on the chalk-board during a lesson can restore the attention of the class. Many vague statements can be made clear by using the chalk-board for sketches, outlines, diagrams, directions and summaries. The chalk-board, used as the occasion demands, throughout a lesson, enables children to see what they have heard.

The chalk-board can be used for quizzes. These may be written on the board before the class arrives. Under such conditions the board should be covered with some wall map or similar substitute to permit all students to quiz at the same time. The quizzes may be planned regarding important persons, events, duties etc. Filmstrip may be flashed on the chalk-board during lessons. Pupils may go to the board and underline or encirele selected items with a chalk. The image on the baord is stable until the projector is shut off. Such a procedure provides variety and is easier than copying so many words or sentences.

The chalk-board can be used for presenting facts, prepared by genealogical tables, listing questions, problems, sources and references, and making assignments. The chalk-board may become the medium through which group projects are worked out. They can be illustrated and summarised by means of chalk-board techniques.

Important Points in Using the Chalk-Board. The following points will aid in the effective use of the chalk-board as a visual aid:

(1) Keep the chalk-board clean. A clean board eliminates needless distractions and makes writing on it easily read from all parts of the room.

(2) Write in straight rows starting at the top left corner.

(3) Make your letters and drawings large enough to be seen from all parts of the room. Cramping your letters, or diagrams cramps teaching. Letters to be seen at thirty feet, ought to be about two-and-a half inches in height.

(4) Plan ahead what you will write on the chalk-board, but draw a map beforehand or by constant reference to a book, as these may give the impression that map drawing is a difficult task.

(5) Get together everything you need for the chalk-board before the class begins—chalk, rulers, T-square, compass,

protractor, stencils or any other device which may help you draw. Use coloured chalk for clearity, emphasis and contrast.

(6) Do not cover up the material on the chalk-board by standing in front of it. Use a pointer.

(7) Talk facing the class. Talking to the students with your back to the class will lose your audience.

(8) Make sure that the chalk-board is not high above the eye-level of the children. The lower half should be skipped over. Make sure that it is well lighted by natural or artificial means, and that the front row of desks is at least eight feet away from it.

(9) Put complex matter on the board before the class meets. Do not waste time by drawing after the opening bell.

(10) Give a good shape to what you write. Shabbily phrased outlines or topics handicap both learner and teacher. Chalk-board exposition should be organised in simple, manageable easily worded units.

(11) Occasionally, a dramatic visual presentation can be made by preparing the entire chalk-board in advance and covering it with strips of paper which will be removed one by one as the demonstration proceeds.

(12) Use your pupils as assistants. Students will enjoy making some of the drawings and outlines; they will learn from doing. The common concentration of teachers and pupils can turn the writing board into a quietly potent unifying force.

(13) Make sure that chalk-board is periodically served.

Types of materials that should go on the board. The following types of materials can go on the board:

(1) A key date, a key personality, a key event, very large figures, to refer to frequently during a period.

(2) Timelines or parts of a timeline on a period or country.

(3) Maps of various kinds, drawn by the teacher or by students.

(4) Materials from which students are to make choices.

(5) Questions for a unit of work.

(6) Summaries of class-work sometimes complied as the discussion develops sometimes written after the discussion.

BULLETIN BOARD

A device of great value for the teaching of history the bulletin board helps the teacher to introduce new facts and ideas to the class and emable the pupils to work as a group and to share their learning experiences. It serves as a place for the display of pictures, drawings, compositions, posters, photographs, news clippings, etc. It provides opportunities for the children to work as a group. It provides in outlet for their creative and artistic testes. It should be fixed at a conspicuous place in the history room easily accessible to and approachable to the students. Materials should be arranged in an attractive and artistic manner, taking into consideration unity and simplicity, attractive lay-out and planning, colour harmony, appropriate captions and interest of the pupils.

FLANNEL BOARD

An important device commonly used in the teaching of history it resembles the black board in shape but its surface is covered with a rough flannel-like cloth, usually grey, black or dark blue in colour. Used by the teacher to place various objects such as pictures, magazine or news-paper 'cut-outs', drawings, text material and other materials in the presentation of the lesson, it adds dynamism to the process of teaching by allowing prepared matter to be brought before the class instantaneously and dramatically. It can be used as an effective teaching device to teach the expansion of an empire. As the unit proceeds, the different parts of the empire cut-out of a large map, may be effectively shown while teaching the expansion of Maratha power or the growth of British empire different parts of the country may be easily displaced on the flannel board in sequential order.

Time lines of a particular period or a movement can be systematically and gradually displayed on the flannel board, clippings, pictures, photos, charts, graphs and other materials can also be displaced to illustrate the economic, social and political aspects of the history of a country.

FILMS

A single picture is effective but pictures presented in sequence have a cumulative effectiveness. They enrich learning by presenting a series or sequences of meaningful experiences involving motion. They can enlarge or reduce the actual size of objects and present processes that might not otherwise be possible to duplicate. They are innately attention getting, generally heighten interest and motivation and offer a satisfying authentic experience based upon dramatisation and emotional appeal. They can transcend the barriers of time, complexity and space and bring the past, present and probable future into the classrroom. They heighten reality by individualising experiences of the outside world and promote a greater understanding of abstract relationships and concepts.

A number of types of films can be used in the teaching of history—films giving information, films dramatising an event, episode or the life of an individual.

In history, instructional films, as Mughal Glory, Six Years of Freedom, etc., documentary films as Unknown Freedom Fighters, Khajuraho, etc., and newsreels presenting in simple descriptive terms the current events are useful. In addition to these, certain commercial films as *Andolan, Mughal-e-Azam, Jhansi Ki Rani, Haqeekat, Kalidas, Johar in Kashmir, Pukar, Sikander, Rustam Sohrab, Humayun, Babar, Jahan Ara, Noorjehan, Tipu Sultan, Razia Sultan, Gandhi* are quite useful.

There are certain limitations to the use of films. The effective use of the film requires special skill and knowledge in the use of projection equipment. The scheduling of appropriate films and equipment is often difficult and time-consuming. Also, it does not by itself enable the student to participate actively in the learning experience. These are the problems to be guarded against.

Radio

Radio is one of the auditory devices which may be utilised for teaching history. It enables the students to listen to the expert, the historian, the author and the first-rate teacher. It can transcend distance and enable the people to hear personalities who are shaping history and thus lend a sense of reality to history. It enables the pupils to be conversant with current history; he feels himself an important part of current history.

There are many types of radio programmes—the school broadcast, the light programme and the general broadcast. Out of these, the school broadcasts are specially meant for the pupils and are relayed during school hours. In these broadcasts, talks and plays on historical topics may be broadcast. There may be systematic talks on national history suited to different classes.

For taking the maximum advantage from the broadcasts, it is very necessary that the teacher creates an atmosphere which is conductive to instruction through radio. He should select those radio lessons which are meaningful to the students and contribute to the study of history. Radio lessons, to be useful, should be integrated with instruction.

The aim of introduction is to stimulate the curiosity of the students. The teacher can give some information about the programme or write some important point about the programme on the blackboard or indicate on the relevant work, map or other aid. He should give a suitable background before the broadcast. A radio lesson can prove effective if it contains something the students never knew before. This will give great satisfaction at the prospect of learning a new fact, getting a new idea or reinforcing an old one.

During the broadcasts, use of visual aids like maps, models, pictures, etc., should be made. Signficant words and statements should be written on the chalk-board. These will help in making broadcast an "audio-visual" experience. Listening should be an active process for the students.

In the follow-up work, the teacher may consolidate the learning gained by the pupils, by briefly reviewing what was presented in the broadcast. The teacher should help the pupils in removing their doubts and clearing the misunderstanding, if any.

Filmstrips

A filmstrip is a series of related still photographs on a single roll of processed film. Taken together, the separate pictures present some process or product learning in stages. Most filmstrips are 35 millimetres. The average number of single pictures on a filmstrip is thirty-five, although the number can vary from ten to one hundred. They may or may not contain captions or titles. They may be produced in black and white or colour and are sometimes accompanied by soud recordings which carry narration, music and sound effects.

The filmstrip possesses many advantages. It allows for student participation either during the actual showing or switching off at intervals to engage in discussion. Unlike the motion picture, the image can be retained on the screen as long as desired. It is inexpensive. It is small and compact.

A wonderful series of 20 filmstrips—Bring India to Your Classroom—has been produced by the All Morrin Studio, Bombay. Some filmstrips in the series—India in the Making, Historical Delhi, Landmarks of India, Festivals of India—are very useful.

❐

7

History Textbook and Supplementary Material

W.H. Burton thinks that a history textbook should be a "useful adjunct to the efforts of the teacher and a reassurance to the pupils." It has a close relationship between the persons and agencies involved in the education of a learner. It has interactions with persons like the learner himself, the teachers, the parents, the supervisors, the curriculum constructors, the text book writers, etc. and with the agencies like schools, the Department of the Boards of Secondary Education, the textbook agencies etc.

According to Webster's Dictionary, 'A manual of instruction, a book containing a presentation of the principle of the subject used as a basis of instruction...'

According to Bacon, 'A book designed for classroom use, carefully prepared by experts in the field and equipped with the usual teaching devices.'

According to Encyclopaedia of Educational Research, "In the modern sense and as commonly understood, the textbook is a learning instrument usually employed in schools and colleges to support a programme of instruction. In ordinary usage, the textbook is printed, it is non-consumable, it is hardbound, it serves an avowed instructional purpose, and it is placed in the hands of the learner."

Importance of a Textbooks

1. An Important Tool for the Teacher. It assists the teacher to plan his daily lesson, prepare assignmens and organise class activities.

2. An 'Assistant Master in Print'. It is content plus instructional technique. It aims at enabling the content understandable to the pupils even in situations where they are not helped by the teacher.

3. Has a Structured Framework. Not essentially based on some pre-determined syllabi which circumscribe the limits of a textbook besides setting the standards at which it has to be written, a textbook spells out and interprets the syllabus for the students and teachers.

4. An Instrument of Some Instructional Objectives. As an important tool of instruction, a textbook is an instrument for the achievement of predetermined objectives.

5. A Self-teaching Device. It enables a student to learn through his own efforts. It provides an opportunity to a student to reflect and evaluate. Without listening to extraneous material that comes before and after it is student can find the specific information he needs in a book. He can review material he has read from time to time to clear up uncertainties.

6. A Constant Companion of a Student. It guides the students in learning—in school and at home. He uses it continuously and constantly. Each word of the textbook has not to be read by every student and he is also expected to understand it.

7. Provides Logical and Comprehensive Material. By providing material in a systematic and comprehensive form a good textbook, sets a standard of minimum essential to be achieved by students of all categories. It provides essential knowledge at one place which teachers are not in a position to dig up.

9. Revolutionise Society. It is used not only for preserving the cultural heritage but also revolutionising a society, its values, beliefs and social systems.

10. Serves as a Laboratory. It enables a student to reinforce the classroom learning, to do assignments at home, to prepare for the examination and to seek guidance and reference for further studies. it provides a common basis on which the process of reading, analysing, outlining and summarising can be mastered.

11. Serves as a Rallying Point. By providing a common ground for both the teachers and the students, it focuses attention on the same issues, events, sequences and circumstances.

12. Serves as a Basis for Almost All the Methods. Almost all the methods of teaching like the assignment, unit method, discussion and the project method can be used with advantage with the help of a textbook.

13. Generates Educational Interaction. It plays a crucial role in generating educational interaction in the classroom between the teacher and the learner, and also between the learner and other co-learners as a result of which learning occurs in a group.

14. Gives Definite Information. It is a storehouse of basic and definite information needed for learning experiences of different kinds. Its use can help the pupils to sum up all the ideas of the unit, acquaint them with the vocabulary, help them learn enough about the topic, to be able to proceed intelligently.

15. Serves as a Syllabus *de facto*. Defining and delimiting his content of teaching a teacher uses the textbook as a prime instructional aid to generate a variety of educative experiences through group work and individual assignments.

CHIEF CHARACTERISTICS OF A GOOD HISTORY TEXTBOOK

(1) Suitable Instructional Objectives. (i) Considering the mental maturity of the students, a good history textbook provides for instructional objective which are:

(a) Attainable.

(b) Practicable.

(c) Worthwhile.

(d) Measurable.

(ii) The instructional objectives contained in the history textbooks should stress:

(a) Achievement of national and emotional integration.

(b) Development of moral and social values.

(c) Acceleration of the process of modernisation.

(iii) Good Textbook includes objectives which facilitate:

(a) Acquisition of knowledge of chronology, concepts, events and facts related to the study of history.

(b) Development of time sense.

(c) Development of historical thinking components of which are:

(i) Analysis.

(ii) Interpretation.

(iii) Comparison.

(iv) Distinguishing.

(v) Drawing inferences and generalisation.

(vi) Weighing of evidence.

(vii) Forming hypotheses.

(viii) Judging and evaluating etc.

(d) Development of certain practical skills like drawing of maps time lines and making of models etc.

2. Organisational Pattern. Good textbook adopts a combination of chronological development of all aspects and thematic approach.

3. Appropriate Approach to the Subject. Good textbook incorporates developmental approach at the elementary and middle classes and socilogical approach with a bias of evolutionary interpretation at the secondary and senior secondary stage.

4. Selection of Contents. (i) Contents contained in the textbooks should be accurate in terms of:

(a) Concepts.

(b) Dates.

(c) Examples.

(d) Events.

(e) Facts

(f) Personalities.

(ii) Good Textbook contains adequate material in terms of the examples and evidences for internalising major ideas.

(iii) Good Textbook contains such material as it caters to the needs of all types of pupils *i.e.* the weak, the average and the bright, etc.

(iv) Contents of good textbook include up-to-date knowledge in terms of:

(a) Controversies.

(b) Findings.

(c) Opinions.

5. Fitness into Total Curriculum. The topics contained in a good textbook have continuity from the preceding stage and should be well articulated.The topics fit into the overall structure not only of the subject but also of the curriculum.

6. Coverage of the Syllabus. Good Textbook contains the material which adequately covers the entire syllabus, all the topics and major ideas. It delineation of the syllabus in accordance with the mental maturity of the students. No redundant material should find place in a textbook.

7. Adoption of the emotional and national integration perspective.

(i) Controversial topics or materials is not included at the elementary and middle classes.

(ii) Balanced view is given of the controversial topics at the secondary and senior secondary topics.

(iii) Controversial topics of issues are viewed in correct historical perspective.

(iv) Good Textbook does not unduly eulogise the culture of the region or condemn the culture of another region.

(v) Good Textbook does contain material which fosters emotional and national integration.

(vi) Good Textbook views the local and regional histories against the background of the history of the country as a whole.

8. Adoption of the Concept of Human Society. (i) Good Textbook views the content of the history of the country against the background of the world history.

(ii) Good Textbook contains the material which reflects the struggle of man to live in an orderly manner in spite of the conflicts and clashes.

(iii) Contents of good textbook inculcate the attitude of respect to and critical appreciation of one's own culture and heritage and of other nations also.

(iv) Contents of good textbook reflect all the aspect of human activities in cultural, economic, political and social fields.

9. Conformity to the Principles of Learning. (i) Material included in good textbooks is in accordance with the principles of simple to complex, concreate to abstract, definite to indefinite and observation to reasoning, etc.

(ii) New knowledge is associated with the previous knowledge.

(iii) Suitable examples is provided so that interest of the students is sustained in the textbooks.

(iv) Contents induces the teachers to adopt suitable methods of teaching.

(v) The uniit plan and the chapter plan is suitable to the age group.

(vi) Content is arranged in such a way as the students lare led to think and reason out critically.

10. Organisation and Presentation of the Material. (i) Organisation of chapters in good textbook is logical.

(ii) Chapters are of appropriate length.

(iii) Chapters are given suitable headings.

(iv) Sub-topics are properly captioned.

(v) Length of the paragraphs is appropriate.

(vi) Organisation of material in a chapter is in logical order *i.e.* first introduction, then body of the material and lastly conclusion. The material is arranged in such a manner as discussion on one aspect leads to another in proper sequence.

11. Suitable Language. (i) Textbook includes the vocabulary, sentence structure, idioms and phrases which are within the comprehension of the students.

(ii) Style employed is effective.

(iii) Structure of the sentences, spelling and punctuations is correct.

12. Illustrations. (i) Good Textbook includes illustrations relevant to the text material.

(ii) The size the type of illustrations included in good textbook suit the age group of the students.

(iii) Colour and lines in the illustrations cater to the interest of the children and are according to their metal maturity.

(iv) The subject in the illustrations is accurate and checked from authentic sources.

(v) The number of illustrations is adequate and covers important and significant text material.

(vi) The space given to the illustrations is good textbook is appropriate.

(vii) Illustrations are vivid.

(viii) Illustrations are of different varieties.

13. Suitable Exercises. (i) Good Textbook includes exercises to text.

(a) Knowledge.

(b) Unerstanding.

(c) Critical thinking.

(d) Skill.

(ii) Good Textbook includes exercise on all the significant areas.

(iii) Exercises give proper weightage to each objective.

(iv) Exercises given are useful for:

(a) Reviewing.

(b) The strengths and weaknesses of the students is diagnosed.

(c) Recapitulating.

(d) The Lesson are developed.

(e) The achievement of the students is Tested.

(v) Textbook includes various forms of questions which are in accordance with the nature of the objective tested. Short answer, essay type, multiple choice, etc. are included.

(vi) Language of the questions is clear.

(vii) Good Textbook includes construction projects and activities for the students.

(viii) Good Textbook includes suitable home assignments.

14. Hints for Teacher. (i) A Good textbook contains hints for teachers in terms of:

(a) Methodology and technology of teaching.

(b) Teaching aids.

(c) Exercises.

(ii) It includes/references for further reading.

(iii) It includes some extracts from original sources.

(iv) It includes glossary and indices.

15. Physical Features of Textbooks. (i) Attractive Get up.

(ii) Good Quality of the paper

(iii) Attractive Cover design

(iv) The Size is handy for the students

(v) Clear Printing

(vi) Proper margins

(vii) Appropriate length of lines

(viii) The types of the print is suitable to age groups of the students

(ix) Uniform Readings

(x) Uniform cost

DEMERITS OF TEXTBOOKS

1. They tend to dominate the educative process. They influence the purpose, character and scope of the curriculum. They dominate the method of instruction and the evaluating process. They narrow down the scope of the curriculum.
2. They do not provide for direct experiences. The students get readymade knowledge and therefore fail to assimilate it properly.
3. Introducing uniformity and rigidity for definite achievements, kill all initiative and spirit of both the pupil and the teacher.
4. A textbook may be used for the purpose of indoctrination of the ideas and beliefs of the party in power. In many countries textbooks have been used for the propagation of fascist and communistic ideas.
5. They are a great hindrance in the new methods of teaching like the Hcuristic and the Inductive. The students get readymade answers this defects the very purpose of as introducing new methods.

History Text-book and Its Importance

Before the script was introduced and the press came into existence, history was taught through 'Oral Method'. The teacher used to convey knowledge verbally and the students used to acquire it through the medium of ears. He utilised the opportunity of using eyes as and when provided. With the introduction of script and the press, the task of the complication and preparation of books came into being. It is said that Comentious is the father of text-book writing. He was the first to have written a book for the teaching of the language. It was the who laid stress on the use of text-books at every stage of education.

French Revolution played a vital role in the introduction of text-books in education. Leaders of revolution thought that it was very necessary to use text-books for teaching. Later on, the text-books of history were written and preapred on behalf of the State. They were intended to inclulate in the citizens loyalty for the leaders of the revolution and faith in the ideals of the revolution besides making the students to memorize historical events.

Later on, America adopted this method. Books were written there with the objective of inclucating faith and allegiance in the ideals of the American War of Independence. Since then with the growth in education, text-books have come to occupy an important place in the teaching.

Place of Text-books in the Teaching of History

The importance and the place of text-books in the teaching of history is a controversial issues. Some scholars are of the opinion that as far as possible, text-books should not be used in the teaching of history. On the other hand, other educationists are of the view that teaching should be conducted through the medium of text-books. Johnson says, "The most important aid in the teaching of history is the text-book. It is indeed more than an aid." Both these views are at extremes. Really speaking, it is a 'golden means' that should be resorted to. It other words, text-books should be used that but sparingly and economically. They should be used for strengthening the experiences of the students. They should not be taught like reading books or supplymentary books in the classroom. These books should be with the students and they should be asked to use them at home for revising the lesson that they have been taught in the class. They may lso be encouraged to take help from these text-books for preparing the answers that they have to write out.

Text-books have a utility for students. They develop self confidence in the students and help them to learn to work in systematic and scientific manner. Besides providing them historical data, they also help the students to learn and draw charts and tables.

The teacher should impart knowledge to the students through varbal method. They should not ask the students to read books in the class. The books that are to be used in the classroom should have certain qualities in them. They should have the following qualities in themselves.

QUALITIES AND CHARACTERISTICS OF HISTORY TEXT-BOOKS

Johnson classified the text-books of history into the following three categories:

(a) Precise text-books, (b) Manuals, and (c) Course.

(a) Precise Text-Books. Precise text-books of concise and short nature. They present the skeleton of the data. They are not written in an elaborate and a detailed form.

(b) Manuals. Manuals are the text-books that are just opposite the precise text-books. They are written in a detailed form and present a detailed description of the facts and the data.

(c) Course. Course are the text-books that persent the complete description, of the facts and the details. There is no likelihood of their further improvements. In the manuals, there is some scope for further improvement, but in the course, there is no such scope.

All these types of books must have the following essential qualities. Without them, they shall not be useful for the students.

(1) Relation of Cause and Effect in the Description. In the history text-books, there should be such a description of the facts and the data that it may seem to be the best on the Law of Causation or cause and Effect. It is not at all wise to give a brief and concise description of the events.

(2) Diction in the Books should be in Accordance with the Requirements of the Age and the Standard. The text-books should be prepared such that they should meet the requirements of age and the stage of education of the students. The language and the style should be such that the subject-matter may be intelligible to the students of that age and stage.

(3) Relationship of the Past Events with the Present Social Problems. An Attempt should be made to co-relate the past events with the social problems of the present-day. An attempt should also be made to show the effect of those events on the present day society. There should be a detailed description of all these things. It shall have a useful effect on the students and they shall try to understand things properly.

(4) Quality of Thought and the lucidity of the Style. The author should present the events and the thoughts in a very clear manner. This is possible only when the author has command over the subject. The style should be lucid. Lucidity of the style does not exclude the literary touch. The style should be simple, but attractive and comprehensive.

(5) Interesting Treatment of Subject-Matter. The subject-matter of the history books should be treated in an-interesting style. The facts and events should be so presented that they may satisfy the curiosity of the students and also make them interested in reading the text-books.

(6) Good Printing and Get-UP. The printing and the get-up of the history text-books should be good. Unless it is so, the students shall not get interested in the text-books.

(7) Well-Illustrated. The text-books should be well-illustrated. They should be full of requisite illustrations, maps, charts etc. These maps and charts should be drawn neatly and be in an acttractive style. This is very necessary for the text-books meant for the students of lower classes. Students have great liking for pictures and charts and unless the books are so they shall not be of interest to the students at that stage of education.

(8) Able to Inculate the Spirit of Internationalism and world Fraternity. History text-books should aim at inculating in the students the feeling of internationalism and world fraternity besides national integration. This is the highest ideal of the present-day life. History text-books should not develop narrow outlook in the students. Unless the text-books are written with this angle they shall be of little use to the students.

Text-books should be Course and not Manuals

This means that the treatment of the subject-matter should be comprehensive. It should not be so that there may be scope of further addition and alteration or development in it.

Element of Selectivity

While construction curriculum, the principle of selectivity is to be borne in mind. Only such events and facts are selected for inclusion in the curriculum that are helpful for upholding social values and make progressive step. This principle should be borne in mind while writing text-books of history. Such events should in mind while writing text-books that have influenced mankind and are likely to cast greater influence in the present social set-up.

Psychological and Scientific

Text-books of history should be written on the basis of the principles of psychology. They should be scientifically planned and written.

List of Contents and Bibliography

There should be a list of contents in the beginning of the book and in the end, there should be a bibliography. List of contents helps the students in finding out the topics which they want to study without wasting much of their time. Bibliography gives them the subject matter for further study of the subject.

Reasonably Priced and Within the Reach of Common People

Text-books should be reasonably priced. They should be priced such that it may be possible for the common man to purchase them.

Questions at the End

At the end of every chapter, there should be certain questions. These questions should be so designed that they may help the students to recapitulate the topic that they have read. These questions should be psychologically planned and scientifically put.

Not Frequently Changed

There has been a tendancy on the part of publishers and authors to change the books frequently. It plays havoc on the purse of the common man. Many boys cannot get proper education for want of money. Hence this tendency should be curbed.

The content material should be properly graded and the style of the book should be in accordance with the requirements of the age and the standard of education.

The books intended for the use in the primary classes, should be written in Story method. The books intended for the Junior High school classes, should be of narrative type. The narration should be realistic, but the element of story must be there.

The books meant for Higher secondary classes should be written in a manner of fact-telling and in a narrative manner. There is no scope for story-telling at this stage of education.

While judging a book's utility for certain stage of education, the organisation of the subject material, the presentation of the subject-matter, illustration etc. should be kept in mind.

IMPORTANT DATES, DYNASTIES AND BATTLES IN INDIAN HISTORY

B.C.

3000 to1500	– Indus Valley Civilization
1900	– Aryans, Rig Veda
1000 to 600	– Epic Age
623 or 567	– Birth of Gautam Buddha
599	– Birth of Shri Mahavira
544 or 543 or 487	– Death of Buddha
327 or 326	– Alexander's Invasion
322-285	– Megasthenese's Visit to India
261 or 260	– Conquest of Kalinga by Askoka
58	– Beginning of Vikram Era (Calendar)

A.D.

78	– Beginning of Saka Era
320 to 534	– Gupta Period
405	– Visit of Chinese pilgrim Fa-Hieu
629-645	– Visit of Chiense pilgrim Hieum-Tsang.
1000-1026	– Mahamud Ghazni attacks India.
1025-26	– Mahamud Ghazni destroys SomNath Temple.
1191	– First Battle of Tarori.

1192	– Second Battle of Tarori.
1347	– Bahmani Kingdom founded.
1398	– Invasion of Timur Lang.
1469	– Birth of Guru Nanak Dev.
1498	– Vasco-da-Gama discovers the sea route to India.
1526	– First Battle of Panipat; foundation of Mughal Rule in North India.
1556	– Second Battle of Panipat; Accession of Akbar.
1571	– Foundation of Fatehpur Sikri.
1576	– Battle of Haldighati.
1582	– Akbar gives a new faith Din-i-Elahi.
1600	– East India Company established in India.
1627	– Birth of Shivaji.
1648	– Taj Mahal at Agra completed by Shah Jahan.
1658	– Aurangzeb ascended the throne.
1675	– Exeution of Guru Teg Bahadur (9th Guru of the Sikhs.)
1680	– Death of Shivaji.
1707	– Death of Guru Govind Singh.
1765	– *Diwani* of Bengal, Bihar and Orissa granted to the British.
1773	– Regulating Act Passed.

1774	– Birth of Raja Ram Mohan Roy, founder of Braham Samaj.
1780	– Birth of Maharaja Ranjit Singh.
1784	– Pit's India Bill Passed.
1793	– Permanent Settlement in Bengal.
1799	– Death of Tipu Sultan; Ranjit Singh occupied Lahore.
1818	– The last Anglo-Maratha War.
1829	– Prohibition of Sati by Lord William Bentinck.
1835	– Introduction of English as medium of instruction.
1839	– Death of Maharaja Ranjit Singh.
1853	– The first Indian Railway line from Bombay to Thana.
1856	– Birth of Bal Gangadhar Tilak.
1857	– First War of Indian Independence.
1858	– End of East India Company's Rule in India.
1861	– Rabindra Nath Tagore born.
1863	– Swami Vivekananda born.
1869	– Birth of Mahatma Gandhi at Porbundar.
1875	– Rishi Dayananda founded Arya Samaj.
1885	– Indian National Congress founded by A.O. Hume.

1886	– Burma annexed by the British.
1889	– Birth of Jaawahar Lal Nehru.
1905	– Partition of Bengal.
1906	– All India Muslim League formed.
1909	– Morley-Minto Reforms Bill passed.
1911	– Partition of Bengal revoked.
1914	– I World War declared.
1918	– End of I World War.
1919	– The Black Bills passed : Tragedy of Jallianwala Bagh at Amritsar.
1920	– Mahatma Gandhi becomes the leader of Indian National Congress; Bal Gangadhar Tilak dies; First Civil Disobedience Movement in India.
1921	– Chauri Chaura outrage.
1928	– Visit of Simon Commission; Death of Lala Lajpat Rai.
1929	– Congress passes Resolution for Purna Swaraj in Lahore Session.
1930	– The Dandi March by Mahatma Gandhi; First Round Table. Conference in London.
1931	– Gandhi-Irwin Pact; Second Round Table Conference.
1932	– The Communal Award announced by the British Premier Ramsay MacDonald.
1935	– Government of India Act 1935 passed.

1939	– II World War started.
1941	– Subhas Chandra Bose escapes from India; Death of Rabindra Nath Tagore.
1942	– British Cabinet Mission to India; Cripps Proposals.
	– Quit India Resolution passed by the Congress.
1945	– I.N.A. men Trial at Red Fort, Delhi; End of World War II.
1946	– First Meeting of the Indian Constituent Assembly.
1847	– India achieves Independence and Country partitioned.
1948	– Kashmir acceded to India.
1948-50	– Princely States integrated into the Indian Union.
1948	– Assassination of Mahatma Gandhi.
	– Shri C. Rajagopalachari becomes the first Indian Governor-General.
	– Dr. Rajendra Prashad becomes the first President.
1049	– Enactment of the Indian Constitution.
1950	– India becomes a Sovereign Democratic Republic on January 26.
1951	– The First Five-Year Plan launched.
1952	– First Census and First General Elections in Free India.

1953 – Mt. Everest scaled by Sherpa Tenzing and E.P. Hillary.

1957 – Second General Elections; Decimal Coinage introduced.

1961 – Liberation of Goa.

1962 – Third General Elections.

– Chinese attack on India (October 20).

– Dr. Sarvepalli Radhakrishnan elected President.

1963 – Nagaland becomes the 16th Indian State.

1964 – Death of Pt. Jawahar Lal Nehru.

1965 – Pakistan attacks India.

1966 – Tashkent Pact.

– Death of Lal Bahadur Shastri at Tashkent.

– Mrs. Indira Gandhi Elected Prime Minister of India.

– Haryana comes into being.

1967 – Fourth general Elections.

– Dr. Zakir Hussian elected the third President of India.

1969 – V.V. Giri elected President of India.

1970 – Meghalaya inaugurated.

1971 – Himachal Prdesh becomes a State.

– Indo-Pak War; Bangladesh is born.

1972 – Simla Agreement; Death of Rajagopalachari.

1973 – Mysore State renanmed Karnataka and the Union Territory of Lacadive, Minicoy & Amindive islands Laskhadweep.

1974 – India explodes a Nuclear device.

– Fakhruddin Ali Ahmed elected fifth President.

– Sikkim becomes an "Associate State" of India.

1975 – India lauches "Aryabhatta."

– Sikkim becomes 22nd State of the Indian Union.

– State of Emergency declared.

1976 – India and China re-establish diplomatic relations.

1977 – Sixth General Elections; Janata Party gets majority in Lok Sabha; Neelam Sanjiva Reddy elected sixth President of India.

1979 – Moraji Desai resigns as Prime Minister; Charan Singh becomes Prime Minister; Charan Singh resigns (August 20); sixth Lok Sobha dissolved.

1980 – Seventh General Elections; Congress (1) comes to power, Mrs. Indira

Gandhi sworn in as Prime Minister; Sanjay Gandhi dies in an air crash; India launches SLV-3 into Space carrying Rohini satellite.

1982 – Aharya J.B. Kriplani dies (March 19).

– INSAT-IA launched : Giani Zail Singh Elected President of India (July, 15).

– Acharya Vinoba Bhave dies (November 15).

– IX Asian Games inaugurated (November 19).

1983 – CHOGM held in New Delhi.

1984 – Operation Blue Star in Punjab; Rakesh Sharma goes into Space; Smt. Indira Gandhi assassinated, Rajiv Gandhi becomes Prime Minister of India.

1985 – Signing of Rajiv-Longowal Accord on Punjab.

– Sant Longowal killed.

– Assam Accord.

– Mizoram Accord.

– Chinese intrusion into Arunachal.

1986 – Shri R. Venkataraman elected President.

– Bofors Gun and Fair Fax controversies.

1987 – Gorkha Hill Council formed.

– Opposition Jan Morcha Front launched.

– R. Venkataraman becomes the President.

1988 – Seven Opposition parties form a National People's Front, called the Rashtriva Morcha Janata Dal; a new political party is lauched at Bangalore.

– Soviet President Mikhail Gorbachev, pays an official visit to India.

1989 – Ninth Lok Sabha Elections.

– Congress (I) defeated in the Lok Sabha Elections.

– V.P. Singh of the National Front Janata becomes the Prime Minister with the outside support of the Bharatiya Janata Party and Leftist parties.

1990 – Government accepts the Mandal Commission Report and issues Orders for the Reservation of 27 per cent of Central Government jobs for the Backward Classes.

– Country-wide protests against Mandal Commission.

– Ram Janambhoomi-Babri Masjid dispute.

	– Withdrawal of support to the National Front Government by the BJP.
	– Defeat of the V.P. Singh. Government in the Lok Sabha on Confidence Vote.
1991	– Census of India : Population—About 84 Crore.
	– P.V. Narasimha Rao of Congress (I) becomes the Prime Minister (June 21, 1991) after the 10th Lok Sabha Elections.
1996 (May)	– Shri A.B. Vajapayee of BJP becomes the PM.
(June)	– Shri H.D. Deve Gowda of United Front becomes the PM.

IMPORTANT BATTLES IN INDIAN HISTORY

Battle of Hydaspes (Jhelum)—July 326 B.C.

Alexander's invasion on India, Porus was defeated.

War against Seleukos—305 B.C.

Seleukos Nikatopr invaded India but was defeated by Chandra Gupta.

Maurya, Seleukos had to cede four Satrapies—Herat, Kandhar, Kabul and Baluchistan to Chandra Gupta.

Battle of Kalinga—261 B.C.

Ashoka defeated the King of Kalinga after a bloody battle. The terrible loss of human lives caused by this war moved the conqueror so much that he renounced all wars in future.

Battle of Thanesar—1014 A.D.

Mahmud of Ghazni defeated Anandpal, the ruler of Thanesar, Mahmud destroyed many temples and took away hundreds of slaves.

First Battle of Tarian—1991 A.D.

Prithvi Raj Chauhan, the Rajput ruler of Delhi and Ajmer defeated Muhammed Ghori, the Sultan of Ghazni.

Second Battle of Tarain—1192

Muhammad Ghori, the Sultan of Ghazni, defeated Prithvi Raj Chauhan, the Rajput ruler of Ajmer and Delhi. It was a big blow to the Rajput power.

First Battle of Panipat—1526

Babar defeated Ibrahim Lodhi and founded Mughal Empire in India.

Battle of Khanwah—1527

Sher Khan, who later become Sher Shah Suri, defeated Humayun, the Mughal Emperor of Delhi.

Second Battle of Panipat—1556

Akbar and his General Bairam Khan defeated Hemu, Akbar consolidated his position and the Mughals once again become the rulers of India.

Battle of Talikota—1565

Rama Raya, the ruler of Vijayanagar, was defeated by the forces of Ahmadnagar, Golkonda and Bidar. It started the disintegration of the Vijayanagar Empire in the South.

Battle of Haldighati—1576

Rana Pratap, the ruler of Mewar, was defeated by the Mughal forces led by Man Singh.

Battle of Plassey—1757

The British led by Clive defeated Siraj-ud-Daula, the Nawab of Bengal. It laid the foundation of British power in Bengal.

Battle of Wandiwash—1760

Count Lally, the Governor of the French Company in India was defeated by Sir Coote, the Commander of English forces. The dream of the French to establish their rule in India was finally shattered.

Third Battle of Panipat—1761

Ahmed Shah Abdali defeated the Marathas on January 14. The dream of Marathas to become paramount power in India came to naught. It weakened the Mughals and left the field clear for the English.

Battle of Buxur—1774

The English forces led by Munro defeated both Mir Kasim and Nawab of Wazir of Oudh. The Company's rule was consolidated in Bengal.

The Fourth Mysore War—1799

The British forces led by Aruthur Wellesley defeated Tipu Sultan, who died fighting. A of his kingdom, consisting of Kanara and Coimbators, was annexed and the rest restored to the old Hindu dynasty.

Third Maratha War—1817-18

The British forces defeated Peshwa Baji Rao, Apa Sahib Bhosle and Holkar, the Maratha rulers, in different battles. Power of the Marathas was completely crushed and the British become indisputably the supreme power in the whole of India.

The First Sikh War—1845-46

The British forces defeated the Sikh armies of Punjab in the battles of Mudki Ferozeshah, Aliwai and Sobraon. The defeat of the

Sikh armies was largely due to the betrayal of their leaders. The territory between's Satlaj and Beas was annexed by the British.

The Second Sikh War—1848-49

The Battles of Ramanagar and Chilianwala between the British forces and the Sikhs were indecisive However. The Sikhs were defeated by the British in the battle of Gujarat. Punjab was annexed by the East India Company.

First War of India's Independence—1857

Indo-Pakistan War—1965 September.

The War started on 1st September, following the infiltration of Pakistani gerialls into Kashmir, when Pakistan attacked India in the Chhamb Jaurian Sector. India's position was slightly better although the war as a whole was indecisive. Fighting stopped on 23rd September. **Indo-Pakistan War**—1971.

Pakistan attacked India on December 3. India retailiated strongly and forcefully. By 16th December, former East Pakistan had been liberated and Indian troops had occupied more than 5,000 sq. miles of Pakistan territory in Sind, Punjab and occupied Kashmir. Fighting stopped on 17th December when Pakistan accepted India's unilateral offer of cease-fire. It was a decisive war in India's favour. Consequently the Yahya Regine collapsed in Pakistan.

IMPORTANT DYNASTIES IN INDIAN HISTORY

Maurya Dynasty—(322—185 B.C.)

Chandragupta Maurya 322—298 B.C.

Ashoka 273—232 B.C.

Kushan Dynasty—(20—225 A.D.)

Gupta Dynasty—(320—606 A.D.)

Chandragupta 320—330 A.D.

Samudragupta—330—375 A.D.

Chandragupta II (Vikramaditya) 375—413 A.D.

Vardhana Dynasty—(580—647 A.D.)

Harsha Vardhana 506—647 A.D.

The Slave Dynasty—(1206—1290 A.D.)

Qutb-ud-din 1206—1210 A.D.

Iltutmish 1210—1235 A.D.

Raziya Begum 1236—1240 A.D.

Balban 1266—1286 A.D.

Khilji Dynasty—(1290—1230 A.D.)

Ala-ud-din Khilji 1296—1316 A.D.

Tughlaq Dynasty—(1320—1412 A.D.)

Muhammad Tughlaq 1323—1351 A.D.

Firuz Tuglaq 1351—1388 A.D.

Lodhi Dynasty—(1477—1526 A.D.)

Ibrahim Lodhi—1517—1526 A.D.

Mughal Dynasty—(1526—1540 A.D., 1555—1857 A.D.)

Babar 1526—1530 A.D.

Humayun 1530—1540 A.D. & 1555—1556 A.D.

Akbar 1556—1605 A.D.

Jahangir 1605—1627 A.D.

Shahjahan 1628—1658 A.D.

Aurangzeb 1658—1707 A.D.

Bahadur Shah II (Zafar) 1837—1857 A.D.

❐

8

Lesson Plans in History

A lesson-plan is the title given to a statement of the achievements to be realised and the specific means by which these are to be attained as a result of the activities engaged in, during the period. It points out what has already been done, in what direction the pupils should next be guided and helped and what work is to be taken up immediately. "It is the teacher's mental and emotional visualisation of the classroom experience as she plans it to occur." It is, in many ways, the core, the heart of effective teaching.

A lesson-plan should tell very simply the story, the way the teacher intends, rightly or wrongly, to employ children for a given period. What he and they are going to do? This written 'story' should show both sincerity and a plan—a flexible and informal plan.

The "story" of the intended lesson should, however, not look like a story. In one sense, the teacher is playing a role—possibly the chief role in a performance (with no play-acting of course), the plan therefore, should look more like a programme. There should be bold headings and lesser headings indicating the different things that are to go on at different times, who are to do those things—(teacher or children or both) what aids are to be used, and a certain amount, not every word of what is to be said.

Need of Lesson Planning

(1) It develops the possibilities of adjustment in the class-room situations which makes the teaching effective.

(2) Through it the teacher regularly achieves the teaching objectives and processes in the form of complete objectives and processes.

(3) It helps in planning the process of teaching on the basis of class-control, motivation and individual differences.

(4) It helps in recalling every step of curriculum unit.

ADVANTAGES OF LESSON PLANNING IN HISTORY

(1) Based on Previous Knowledge. In preparing lesson plans the teacher presents new knowledge as the basis of previous knowledge of the pupils.

(2) Suitable Environment. Objectives are fixed and the teaching strategies, tactics, teachniques and material aid etc. are decided before-hand in a lesson plan. This creates interest of the pupils in the lesson and helps in creating proper environment of teaching task goes in a very planned way, when a proper teaching environment is created.

(3) Limitation of Subject Matter. The subject-matter becomes limited. It enables the teacher to give up irrelevant material. As he only remembers definite and limited its presentation before the pupils becomes easy.

(4) Psychological Teaching. In preparing lesson plans, the teacher uses proper teaching strategies, teachniques, tactics and instruments keeping in mind the interests, aptitudes, needs, capacities and abilities of the pupils for teaching them. This makes teaching more psychological. The pupils receive the knowledge in a systematic and organized way.

(5) Means for Developing Teaching Skills. The lesson plan acts as an important means for developing teaching skills in the pupil-teachers.

(6) Use of Theoretial Knowledge in Teaching. Theoretial knowledge attained by pupil teachers during their training period, can be applied in the class with the help of lesson-plan. It helps in providing practical shape to the theoretial knowledge.

(7) Determination of Activities. The teacher's and pupils activities are pre-decided in a lesson plan according to the class level. While preparing lesson-plan, the teacher decides what he and his pupils are to do in the class. This makes the teaching activities meaningful and purposeful. Consequently, both the pupil and the teacher become active in developing the lesson.

(8) Preparation of Material Aids. While preparing a lesson-plan, the teacher decides facts are to be clarified, strategies, tactics techniques instruments and aids to the used. It prepares the necessary and effective aid before starting the teaching task.

(9) Orderlines and Development in Thinking. By preparing a lesson plan is reated orderliness and development in the thinking of the pupils enabling the teacher to achieve the teaching objectives while presenting the contents in an orderly way.

(10) Economy of Energy and Time. The preparing lesson plan before-hand the teacher can present the new knowledge in a proper sequence before the pupils and can successfully remove their doubts.

(11) Evaluation Possible. A lesson-plan has the provision of the evaluation. Which makes the teacher aware of how teaching has affected the pupils. It also evaluates the strategies, tactics techniques and aids used by the teacher and he can modify them accordingly. Thus, he can evaluate the teaching strategies, tactics, techniques and instruments and their effects used by him.

(12) Revision of Knowledge. In a lesson-plan, the teacher writes summary of the lesson, the reading of which helps pupils in the revision of the lesson.

(13) Discipline in the Class. By preparing lesson plan, the teacher becomes aware of what, when and how much is to be done in the class. He absorbs all the pupils in their respective tasks. It results in appreciable class-room discipline.

(14) Teaching with Confidence. The preparation of a lesson plan makes the subject of teaching and other alied subjects more clear to the teachers. This arouses self-confidence in the teacher. Now the presents knowledge to the pupils with more enthusiasm and pleasure. This makes the class lively.

AN IDEAL LESSON PLAN IN HISTORY

(1) Based on Previous Knowledge. To avoid any difficulty in acquiring new knowledge by the pupils, an ideal lesson plan should be based on their previous knowledge.

(2) Objective Based. The lesson plan must be based on one or the other objective, written and defined clearly.

(3) Appropriate Material Aids. Correct decision regarding the charts, graphs, pictures, diagrams and maps should be taken while preparing ideal lesson plans, marked at proper places which a teacher is to use while teaching.

(4) Division of Lesson Plan into Units. Lessions are of three types (i) knowledge lessons, (ii) Skill lessons, (iii) Appreciation lessons. All the relevant steps of these three types of lesson plans should be determined in an ideal lesson plan. Each lesson should be divided into suitable units so that the pupils may understand it gradually.

(5) Determination of Activities. It should be made clear what activities a teacher and the pupils are to perform. The activities of a teacher and the pupils should be determined before-hand in an ideal lesson plan.

(6) Use of Illustrations. Examples should be used which have relevance with the daily life of the pupils. This depends upon the comprehensive knowledge and experience of the teacher.

(7) Individual Guidance. The technique and occasion of providing individual guidance to the pupils should be indicated.

(8) Use of Strategies, Tactics, Techniques and Teaching Aids. The teacher should gain the knowledge of maxims of teaching and general principles of teaching. Only then, he can use appropriate strategies or methods, tactics, techniques and aids in order to classify the events and acts which occur in different situations.

(9) Correlation. A possible correlation should occur to enable the pupils to acquire the knowledge as a whole.

(10) Teaching from Memory Level to Reflective Level. Developmental and thought—provoking questions should be asked in an effort to stretch the teaching from memory level to the reflective level.

(11) Time-sense. Lesson plan should be prepared according to the mental level of the pupils and the duration of the periods. The time assigned for every teaching step should be made clear in it.

(12) Use of Black-Board. The black-board summary of each and every unit should be written on the black-board immediately after teaching it in small but complete sentences.

(13) Evaluation. There should be a mention of the method of knowing the influence on the pupils. This involves evaluation of the methods used by the teacher.

PRE-REQUISITIES OF LESSON PLAN IN HISTORY

(1) Clarity of Objectives. There should be clarity of objectives. It will make the both pupils and the teachers active to achieve them.

(2) Knowledge of the Subject. The teacher should know history well for preparing the lesson plan. If they have no clearity about history teachers fail to clarify various facts and events of the lesson. Therefore, pupil-teachers should read the whole lesson plan which they have prepared. They should not read the text-book only, but also read other supplementary books and the available material concerning the topic.

(3) Knowledge of the Principles and Strategies of Teaching. The teacher must know the principles of teaching, maxims of teaching, teaching methods and techniques to enable him to mention the teaching methods and techniques in the lesson plan.

(4) Knowledge of Student's Nature. The teaching method will be advantageous only when the nature of the pupils is known along with knowledge of the subject-matter.

(5) General Knowledge of All Subjects. The pupil teacher should also possess general knowledge of all the subjects, because the knowledge is a complete unit and it cannot be divided into different parts. Hence, to teach any subject properly the teacher must know the other related subjects.

(6) Clarity about Previous Knowledge. The teacher should know the previous knowledge of the pupils because the new knowledge imparted on the basis of previous knolwedge is easily stablized.

(7) Division of Units. The teacher should divide the topic in units. Also, teaching method or strategy should be determined. This simplifies the preparation of the lesson plan. It is acquired easily by both the pupils and the teachers.

(8) Knowledge of Class Level. The teacher should know the class-level for which he is to prepare the lesson plan which some fresh teachers overlook. This disturbs the teaching and the pupils fail to understand anything.

(9) Use of Material Aids. It should be decided at what step the material aid is to be used and what is to be clarified with that aid. This maintains the naturality and interesting feature of the lesson plan.

(10) Flexibility. As the lesson plan is a slave not the master of the teacher, hence, the teacher is free to make changes in the lesson plan in order to create attraction and interest in the lesson.

Principles of Lesson Planning

Below we list some principles which may be helpful in preparing a lesson-plan:

(1) The teacher should prepare a careful but flexible plan. He should be so secure in the plan that he should be free to change it as the developing lesson and needs of the children require. The plan is to be used as a guide rather than as a rule of thumb to be followed blindly. The teacher should have the courage to deviate from it when needs of his children demand.

(2) The teacher must have mastery of and adequate training in the topic from which the subject matter has been selected for a certain lesson.

(3) The teacher must know his pupils thoroughly and organise the materials in a psychological rather than merely a logical fashion. He must understand his pupils' traits and interests in order to know how to provide for them.

(4) The teacher must keep abreast with new methods and techniques of teaching history.

(5) The teacher must ensure active pupil participation.

(6) Since monotony is a drawback, so work during a lesson should be varied, particularly with young pupils. This variety of work may be marked on different stages of the lesson in the same period, by pupils' writing, watching, doing or listening to some person.

Steps in Lesson Planning

For teaching history effectively, the teacher has to proceed in a systematic manner. For this purpose, some steps (although there can be no rigidity about them) have to be followed. Let us now discuss those steps which may help in preparing a lesson plan in history.

Formulation of Educational Objectives (Aims)

As the teacher sists at his desk planning a lesson, he should ask himself these questions:

(i) Is this lesson primarily one of attitudes, skills, concepts, or knowledge? or is it a combination of two or more of these?

(ii) If he can get just one idea or attitude or skill or concept across today, what should it be? What does he want them to know when they leave the classroom? "What is the 'bull's-eye' of the teaching target for today?" as is to well by Leonard Kenworthy.

(iii) What are one or two other major aims? Are these aims suitable for this class or far beyond their level of comprehension? Or possibly behind them?

(iv) Are these aims specific?

He should remember that the specific aims will be determined in their relationship to general aims. He should think out the statement as to what he intends to do in that particular lesson, e.g., to enable the pupils to be familiar with the social, economic and cultural advancement during the Gupta Period.

Selection and Organisation of Content

Now he should ask himself:

(i) What type of content should he select to enable him to achieve the intended objectives?

(ii) How can he use the present knowledge of the pupils to make the lesson meaningful and interesting to the pupils? How can he arrange the relevant facts in order and correlate them with the life of the students?

(iii) How much time be spent in discussion, revision, practical work or in disciplinary interruptions. This will enable him to arrange rate of exposition accordingly.

(iv) How can he start this lesson? Can he use this motivation throughout the lesson?

(v) How can he reach the slow students? How can he reach the fast students?

(vi) What materials or aids can he use best? Are these suitable for all the students?

(vii) How can he summarise the lesson?

(viii) What homework should he give?

Motivation of Preparation

The word motivation is used in two different ways:

1. Motivation as a Broad Approach to Teaching. In this sense motivation includes all that we know about learning. It is something that is going on all through the period. It comes from the teacher's use of his voice, good questioning, by relating the past to the present and from many other sources.

2. Motivation as a Means of Getting a Lesson Underway. In this sense, motivation means ways of getting a lesson started, getting a lesson "of the ground" so to say.

He can motivate the pupils for the new lesson:

(a) **By the Use of Objects.** Costumes, coins, sculpture pieces, pictures, etc., may be used to start a topic.

(b) **By Opening with a Startling Statement or Question.** At the beginning of the lesson, the teacher makes the statement—The Sepoy Revolt of 1857 was the First War of Indian Independence. The rest of the period can be spent in discussing why this statement is true.

(c) **By Using Socio-drama.** The teacher annouunces that he wants volunteers for positions in the court of Aurangzeb. Some pupils may volunteer to pay the role of Aurangzeb, some others may play the role of Shivaji.

In a smilar way, individuals can be selected or asked to volunteer to represent the great freedom fighters. They can then be asked to make brief statements on how they contributed in the struggle for Indian independence. For this type of lesson, an assignment to learn dramatisation should be given to one of the pupils in advance. Throughout the lesson, these roles should be maintained.

(d) **By Posing a Problem.** As soon as the class starts, the teacher says that some recent excavations have been made which have brought to light some human skeletons of Harppan age at a number of places like Chandigarh, Ropar, Lothal, etc. What is your ideas about the extent of Harppan civilisation? The rest of the period can then be spent in discussing the details of Indus Valley Civilisation.

(e) **By Using a Filmstrip or Film.** There are certain very good filmstrips and films available which can be used to motivate the students. The sources of filmstrips and films have been given in Appendix II.

(f) **By Using the Chalk-board.** At the start of the period or before the students have entered the room, the teacher draws a pyramid on the board. Then he suggests that in some way, this represents the Indian people at the time of 1947 when the British were to quit India. During the rest of the period, the class fills in this chart with the names of the leaders, the Prime Minister, Lord Mount-batten, and other leaders. A discussion can be held on how Indians took over the reins of government in their hands.

A word of caution here! Not all the lessons need to have a startling opening. The motivation can come from instrinsic interest aroused in scores of ways over a long period of time. But the techiniques suggested above, and others, have been given to illustrate how teachers can arouse and maintain interest throughout a period.

Students' Activity and Teachers' Role

There should be a fair distribution of time between student's and teacher's activities. The teacher can keep his pupils active by frequent questions—fairly distributed over the whole of the class. The pupils can be encouraged to ask questions. Thus there should be a two-way traffic. As far as possible, the pupils should be active participants in the learning process. From time to time, it is helpful to keep a record of pupil participation:

(i) To see how many questions are coming from pupils.

(ii) To see who is taking too much part in class discussion and who is not taking enough part.

(iii) To see if there is any section or group of students that the teacher is neglecting.

Recapitulation and Assignments

A leason without recapitulation is incomplete. Its principal purpose is to make the presentation more effective. It helps the pupils to come to some conclusion with reference to the wider signficance of the problem. An attempt is made to ask children to "tell back" or reproduce what they have learnt. The pupils learn how to express themselves and to reproduce the material learnt.

Assignment from the topics covered, is essential for the consolidation of knowledge. Let the pupils do some exercise in the form of answers to some question (objective or essay types), draw the maps and indicating the extent of empires or important places, collect the statements, sayings or couplets of great leaders, saints, and prepare scrapbooks, write out reports, etc.

Advantages of the Lesson Planning

We have already seen that planning of the lesson is greatly needed. This planning has following advantages:

(1) If the lesson plan is drawn in advance, the teacher gets an opportunity to cast a glance at the subject that he is going to teach. He goes prepared to the class and the picture of every detail of the lesson is before his eyes.

(2) The teacher is well aware of the previous knowledge or 'knowledge assumed' of his students and so, he can move ahead successfully towards the goal.

(3) If the teaching is imparted through a lesson plan, the knowledge that is imparted to the students, is well organised and systematic. The entire subject-matter shall be presented before the students in the form of a chain of events. The teacher shall go on exciting the curiosity of the students by and shall go on satisfying their knowledge in a successful manner. This shall have good effect on the knowledge of the students.

(4) Knowledge that is imparted through a lesson plan, is clear and effective.

(5) In lesson plan, it is possible for the teacher to move in a scientific manner. The teacher can safely proceed from simple to difficult.

Important of the Lesson Plan in the Training Colleges

Students, when they enter training colleges, have to draw lesson plan. A good deal of their success in the training colleges, depends upon these lesson plans. If the pupil teacher is able to teach his class properly, he is likely to get a good division.

Basic Requirements or Guiding Principles of the Lesson Plan

Lesson plan should be drawn with an eye on the following requirements:

(1) The aim of the lesson plan is to present the knowledge effectively and in a successful manner. The teacher should, therefore, try to correlate the previous knowledge of the students with the present knowledge.

(2) In every lesson plan, the aim of the teacher is to impart new knowledge to the students. The teacher should try, to put up new problems before the students and thus èxcite the power of thinking of the students and later on add new knowledge to their old store.

(3) In the lesson plan, the aim of the teacher should be quite clear. The introduction should draw the attention of the students towards him. The teacher should succeed in making the minds of the students quite active and full of creative knowledge.

Presentation of the subject-matter should also be quite effective and clear. An attempt should be made to co-relate the past knowledge of the students with the present knowledge.

(4) Knowledge can be effective and powerful only if it is put to practical use. The teacher should try to provide an opportunity to the students to put their knowledge to practical use.

(5) The teacher should also put such questions to the students which may facilitate the comparative study of the subject.

(6) The lesson plan should not be very long. It shall be concise and up to the mark.

(7) The teacher should try to give a good deal of opportunity for application and practical use in the lesson plan.

(8) There should be proper place for recapitulation in the lesson plan. If the lesson is long, the students should be provided with several opportunities for recapitulations.

(9) The presentation of the subject-matter is very important step of the lesson plan. Presentation is made with the help of various aids. If the presentation is successful, then only the subject-matter can be put effectively. Pupil teacher should try to make presentation lively and interesting.

(10) In drawing lesson plan, the teacher should test the previous knowledge of the students through certain questions.

(11) Every step of the lesson plan should be well organised and systematic. It should be balanced as well.

(12) Blackboard work is an essential part of lesson plan. It should be properly organised.

If the lesson plans are drawn with these things in view, the pupil teachers are sure to get success.

Given below is a model of lesson plan.

LESSON PLAN

Draw a 'Lesson Plan' for Class IX. This plan should be intended to teach the students that Warren Hasting's internal policy was a blot on the history of British rule in India.

Name of the Institution —Mahatma Gandhi Higher Secondary School, Varanasi.

Teaching method —Story method (Through question-answer).

Name of the Pupil Teacher —Bhagwati Prasad Rastogi.

Date — August 8, 1978.	Period — Fourth.
Class — IX	Time — 40 Minutes.
Subject— Condemnable works of Warren Hastings	Average age— 15 years.

General Aims

(1) To develop amongst the students the curiousity to know and thereby develop their intelligence and character.

(2) To acquaint the students with the knowledge of history and thereby develop their intelligence and character.

(3) To develop in the students the sense of patriotism by acquainting them with the deeds and lives of great men of their country.

(4) To develop amongst the students the ability to discuss and present the matter in an appealing way.

Specific Aims

(1) To acquaint the students with the evil deeds of the British rulers in India.

(2) To discuss condemnable works of Warren Hastings.

Teaching Aids

(1) A Map of India depicting the territory under the British rule.

(2) Other equipments useful for the classroom teaching.

Introduction

In order to introduce the topic, the teacher shall put the following questions to the students:

(1) Who was the founder of British rule in India?

(2) Who was the Second Governor-General of the East India Company in India?

Presentation

Today, we will discuss about those work of Warren Hastings for which he has been condemned by almost all the historians and he became a blot on the British rule in India. Warren Hastings has been condemned for his various deeds. The important amongst them are:

(1) His Rohilla Policy,

(2) His actions against Nand Kumar,

(3) His cruelties on Chet Singh, and

(4) His policy towards the Begums of Oudh.

LESSON PLAN

LIFE UNDER THE GUPTAS

Class VII

Average age of the pupils : 13 to 15 years.

Duration of the Lesson 40 Minuts

Illustrative Material with the Teacher

(1) Ordinary class-room apparatus.

(2) A map of India, showing the extent of Gupta Kingdom.

(3) A map of India, showing the modern administrative divisions of the country.

(4) A picture of coins of Samudra Gupta.

(5) Some pictures of Ajanta Caves.

(6) Some pictures of Hindu Gods and Goddesses.

(7) A picture of the "Iron Pillar" at Mehrauli.

(8) A copy of the "Shakuntala" and a copy of the "Panchtantra"

(9) A map of India, showing the political condition of India on the eve of the establishment of Gupta kingdom.

Objectives of the Lesson.

General

(1) To inculcate a pride in their heritage.

(2) To create an appeciation for the great contribution of their forefathers in the various fields of human activity.

(3) To develop the right attitudes of fellow-feeling, friendliness, co-operation, toleration and international understanding.

(4) To explain that our present Indian social life is not a sudden growth. It has evolved in its various environments through various ages and stages.

Specific

To familiarise with the political, social, economic, religious and cultural life of people under the Guptas.

Introduction

1. Mention the important conquests of Chandra Gupta I
2. Name the important conquests of Samudra Gupta.
3. What were the main conquests of Chandra Gupta Vikramaditya?
4. What was the result of all these conquests?

Announcement of the Aim

Today we shall study not only the political life but also the social, economic, religious and cultural life of the people under the Guptas.

Presentation

The lesson will be divided into three sections as follows—

(a) Political life under the Guptas.

(b) Social and economical life under the Guptas.

(c) Religious and cultural life under the Guptas.

SECTION I

Matter	*Method*
The Gupta kingdom was divided into provinces, know as Desas. Since the decline of the Mauryas, India had been frequently invaded be foreigners like the Greeks, the Parthians and the Sakas. They established their rule in North Western India. In other parts of India were petty native states engaged in mutual warfare. After waging ruthless wars against the northern and southern states, the great Gupta rulers gave political unity to a ıarge part of India and established a strong Central Government.	Explain this point by correlation with the present administrative Illustrates with the help of the map of India, showing the political condition of the country on the eve of the establishment of of Gupta Kingdom. Elucidate with the help of the map of India showing the extent of Gupta Kingdom. Show to pupils, on the map of Gupta Kingdom like Vaisali, Ujjain, Saurashtra and Bengal etc. indicating the extent of Gupta Kingdom.
Gupta's civil and military administration was highly organised. At the top of the administrative system stood the king, the fountain-head of the all the civil, military and judicial administration. He was assisted by a number of ministers in charge of different departments of the Govt. Who controlled the activities of the entire kingdom, concerning their respective departments receiving regular reports and issuing important instructions from time to time.	Gupta King's position correlated with the position of the President of India. The position of Gupta kingdom.

Contd.

Matter	*Method*
The Governor of a province enjoyed the title of a Raja. He generally belonged to the royal family. He was responsible for a good and efficient rule of his province. There was however no rigid separation between civil and military officials. These posts were transferable. The provinces were further subdivied into districts known as Vishyas. The district officer, called Vishyapati, was like the present day District magistrate responsible for maintaining peace and order in his district. A body of four men, representing the four guilds of the town...the bankers, the artisans, the merchants and the literacy classes, assited him in the task of district administration. In each Vishya were a number of villages, called Gramas. There were Village Panchayats for looking after the local administration. The king and other officers under him, went on extensive tours of the country to get first hand information of the condition and life of the people.	divisions of India—states, districts, tehsils and villages. Show the map of India, showing the present day administrative units of the country. correlate with the provincial administration of the Mauryas. Correlate Vishyapati with the present day Deputy Commissioner and other executive officers in district administrative. Who assists the Deputy Commissioner in the task of district administration? Correlate with the modern Panchayat Raj in India., Correlation with the official tours of present day field officers.

Sectional Revision

The following questions will be asked—

1. What was the position of the Gupta kings?
2. How was the country divided for administrative purposes by the Gupta kings?

SECTION II

Matter	*Method*
The people were generally vegetarians in the matter of diet. The followed the principles of Ahimsa. There were no wine shops and distillaries. Only the Chandals, which were the most degraded class, killed animals and ate meat. They lived outside the towns and villages. When they entered the city of the market, they had to strike a piece of wood so that other people might not come in contact with them. Common people even did not take onion and garlic. They lived a high moral life. They were honest, generous, charitable and hospitable. There was plenty to eat and spare. There were big free hospitals for the poor at their own expenses. Fahien says that people were law-abiding, taxes were light, roads were safe and there system. Cowries and shells were the usual medium of exchange. Gold Sayorns and silver dinars were also in circulation. Criminal law was very mild. This is a sure proof of the peace loving and	Elucidate by telling that it was all due to the influence of Buddhism, partronised by great Indian Kings like Ashoka and Kanishka. Correlate with the present policy of prohibition of the Govt. of India. Tell there are any such distinction in our society these days. Correlate with the present casteless society of Indian people from Government point of view. Correlate with the present day moral standards of our people. Correlate with the severity of criminal law, strict official regulations and the hateful and oppressive spy system of the Mauryan days with Gupta administrative system which was both mild and efficient. Show pictures of the gold coins of Samudra Gupta. Correlate with present day sources of income

Contd.

Matter	*Method*
civilized ways of the people. Land revenue the main source of income of the state fixed at a certain portion of the produce, it could be paid in cash or kind. The royal officers received fixed salaries. Agriculture, arts and crafts were in flourishing condition.	of the Govt. of India as well as those of the state governments.

Sectional Revision

1. What was the economic condition of the people under the Guptas?

2. Describe briefly the social life of the people, living in those days.

LESSON PLAN

Class : VI

Unit : Mauryan Empire

Topic : Life under the Mauryas.

Aids: (1) A map of India showing the extent of Mauryan Empire.

Right of coinage vested in State.

SECTION III

Matter	*Method*
Architecture and Art—Pillars, stupas and rock caves formed an important part of architectural	What do you know about the progress of art and architecture during this period?

Contd.

Matter	*Method*
work. Stupas of Sanchi-Practice of engraving on stone.	
Persian influence on architecture. Stone dressing and Polishing a unique feature—great patronage to art by the Mauryas.	What influence was quite distinct on architecture during this time?

SECTION IV

Language : One common language for the whole empire attempted—Asokan inscriptions in Bali—this promoted cultural unity.

Recapitulation or Evaluation: (1) Dramatise the role of Megasthenes presenting the report of the Indian people to an audience of Greeks.

(2) Identify points of similarity and difference between the life of the people in cities and villages in Mauryan times and now.

Home Assignment: (1) The pupils may be asked to write a short essay on the social and cultural life of the people during the Mauryan age.

(2) The pupils may be asked to draw an outline map of India and indicate the extent of Mauryan kingdom along with its important towns.

Chalkboard Work

1. Social conditions: Caste system—ascendancy of Brahmanism—joint family system—education, religious in character.

Food—use of rice, barley, wheat and milk.

2. Economic Condition. Economic life controlled by the state village, the unit of agricultural life—sources of revenue—land, water cess—state monopoly in industries. State control of prices—trade taxed—import and export duties—right of coinage vested in state.

3. Architecture and art: Pillars, stupas, and rock-cut caves. Persian influence on architecture.

4. Language : One common language Pali.

Suggested References for Teachers

1. Chandragupta Maurya and His Times, by Radha Kumund Mukerjee, pp. 183-225.
2. The Age of Imperial Unity. Vol. III, Bharatiya Vidya Bhawan. pp. 542-610.
3. Asokan Inscriptions, Radha Govind Basak (Rock Edict VI, p. 35).
4. Ancient India as Described by Megasthenes and Arrian by M.C. Crindle.
5. Asoka and the decline of Mauryas by Romila Thapar pp. 55-93.

LESSON PLAN

Class—VII B

Average Age of the students—11 years

Topic—Babar's Conquest of Delhi

Time—40 minutes

Illustrative Aids

(i) A map of India showing territories conquered by Babar.

(ii) Sketch of the First Battle of Panipat.

(iii) A chart showing weapons of war used in medieval and modern time.

(iv) Ordinary class-room apparatus.

Objectives for Students

(1) General

(i) To acquaint with the medieval History of India and to show that present is the outcome of the past.

(ii) To develop historical imagination and reasoning and to incluate partriotism.

(iii) To acquaint with the personal qualities of Babar as a general.

(2) Specific. To understand how Babar captured Delhi.

Previous Knowledge

As the students have already read upto the end of Lodhi dynasty they are prepared for the study of the First Battle of Panipat, fought between Ibrahim Lodhi and Babar.

Motivation

In order to know the depth of previous knowledge of the students, the pupil-teacher first of all, will draw the map of India on the black-board and ask the following questions—

(i) Which is the capital of India?

(ii) Which is the historical battle-field near Delhi?

(iii) Between whom was the First Battle of Panipat fought?

Statement of Aim

Today we shall discuss how Babar conquered Delhi.

Presentation

The lesson will be divided into two units.

FIRST UNIT

Matter	*Method*
Zahir-ud-Din Muhammad Babar was born in 1483 A.D. At his age of twelve, his father Sultan Umar Shaikh Mirza died and he became the king of Farghana, which is now a small province of Russina Turkistan. He wanted to conquer Samarkand, but due to the intrigues of his relatives he also lost Farghana. Luckily for him a rebellion occurred and he occupied Kabul in 1504 A.D. He assumed the title of Badshah The Emperor. He made some unsuccessful attempts to regain his patrimony. Being disappointed Babar truned his attention towards India between 1519, and 1526. He invaded India five times the battle of Panipat was the last of these attempts. The following were the causes that tempted Babar to conquer India— (i) His strong ambition to conquer India. (ii) Poplitical condition of India. (iii) Unpopular Government of Ibrahim I odhi.	(i) Where is Farghana in the map? (Map will be shown) (ii) Who was Babar's father? (iii) What was his aim when he ascended the throne of Farghana? (iv) How did Babar lose Farghana? (v) How did Babar capture Kabul? (vi) What was the age of Babar when he set up a kingdom in Kabul? (vii) Why did Babar make up his mind to conquer India? (viii) What was the political condition of India on the eve of Babar's invasion? Show map of India in 1526 A.D.

Contd.

Matter	*Method*
(iv) Internal feud among the Chiettains.	
On the Invitation of Daulat Khan, the governor of the Punjab in 1524 A.D., Babar invaded Punjab but soon returned to Kabul.	(ix) Why did Babar invade Punjab?
Babar was eager for the conquest of Hindustan. Punjab easily fell into his hands, but to conquer Delhi was a more difficult task.	(x) Why did Babar invade Punjab again?
Babar's approach was welcomed by the discontented elements in the country. He also received a message of help from Rana Sanga of Mewar who he afterward accused of the non-fulfilment of his promise.	(xi) Why did the people welcome Babar? (xii) Why did Rana Sanga promise to help Babar?
Hearing the news of Babar's approach Ibrahim sent his two advance parties to deal with him but both the them were defeated. Babar advanced towards Delhi. Ibrahim came out of Delhi to wage battle. The opposing armies met on the historic plain of Panipat.	(xiii) What did Ibrahim do, when he heard about Babar's advance to Delhi?

Sectional Recaptulation

(i) What do you know about the early life of Babar?

(ii) Why did Babar want to conquer India?

(iii) What was the condition of India on the eve of Babar's inasion?

(iv) Where did the two armies meet?

FIRST UNIT

Matter	*Method*
With the help of his able generals Babar organised his artillery in the front, assisted by an organised cavalry of 13000. He took a highly advantageous position to encounter with the enemy.	(i) How did Babar organise his forces in the battle-field?
Sultan Ibrahim's army was estimated to be about 100000 soldiers and 100 elephants. As was not a good general, he could not organise his army properly.	(ii) How did Ibrahim Lodhi organise his forces? Show sketch of the battle-field.
The two armies faced each other for eight days, but neither side took the offensive. At least Babar's patience was exhausted and he resolved on a prompt action. The battle raged firercely on 21st April, 1526. Attacked with arrows and artillery the Afghans were hemmed in on all sides and Ibrahim's army was utterly defeated. Ibrahim died fighting like a valient Afghan. The success of Babar was due to his veteran generalship and arrangement of cavalry and	(iii) What were the weapons of war used by Babar and Ibrahim Lodhi? To create time sense among the students, ask them to tell the weapons of war used in the modern age. Show chart of modern and medieval weapons. Who won the battle? What were the causes of Babar's success?

Contd.

Matter	*Method*
artillery. Ibrahim was not a good general. He could not organise his army efficiently. Babar was fortunate enought to avail himself of the servies of skilled generals.	
The battle of Panipat placed the empire of Delhi in Babar's hands. The power Lodhi dynasty was shattered. The sovereignty of Hindustan passed into the hands of Mughals.	What were the results of the first battle of Panipat?

Sectional Recapitulation

(i) How did Babar organise his forces in the first battle of Panipat?

(ii) How did Babar get success?

(iii) What were the results of the first battle of Panipat?

Final Recapitulation

(i) What was the political condition of India on the eve of Babar's invasion?

(ii) What were the causes of Babar's success in the first battle of Panipat?

(iii) What were the results of the first battle of Panipat?

Black-Board Summary

Write important points on the black-board.

Home Tasks

What were the factors that contributed to the success of Babar in the first battle of Panipat?

LESSON PLAN

Class—VII

Topic—Maharana Pratap

Time—40 Minutes

Average Age 12 Years

Illustrative Aids

1. A map of India

2. Time Chart

3. Pictures-Rana Partap on Chetak, Akbar, Scene of the battle of Haldi Ghati, Rana crossing the Nullah, Rana Pratap and his family in hills. Bhama shah giving wealth to Pratap.

Objectives

1. **General—**As usual

2. **Specific—**To familiarise the students with the life of Maharana Pratap and his struggle for the freedom of his Native State.

Previous Knowledge

The student's knowledge about the Mughal Kings and the Rajputs. They will be used during the course of the lesson.

Introduction : Show the map of India and ask following questions:

1. What was the extent of the empire of Akbar?

2. Indicate the location of Rajputana and its important cities.

Statement of the Aim

Today we shall study about the brave deeds of Maharana Pratap.

Presentation

Matter	*Method*
1. Rana Pratap Son of Uday Singh and brother of Shakti Singh succeeded his father to throne of Udaipur in 1572. Akbar made friendship with most the important Hindu rulers; with some by matrimonial alliance and with some force. Even the brother of Pratap, Shakti Singh submitted himself to Akbar. However Pratap brave Rajput with keen sense of self-respect never surrendered to Akbar.	1. Show the picture of Rana Partap and the time chart. 2. Show Picture of Akbar. 3. Ask students to locate Udaipur on the map of India.

Recapitulation

1. When did Rana Pratap ascend the throne?
2. How did Akbar make friendship with Hindu rulers?

❐

9

Presentation of History at Different Stages

Once the Subject matter of history has been selected and arranged, the question of presenting it before students arises. The teacher shall have to employ certain methods for the presentation of subject-matter before the students of different classes. These methods shall differ according to the age of students and their class. In spite of these differences, there are certain fundamentals that have to be kept in mind, presenting the subject matter before the students. A few of them are being enumerated below:

(1) In the classroom, the teacher should try to present fact in a simple. Intelligible and effective manner. Preciseness always pays.

(2) There is very little scope for discussion and presentation of the differences of opinion in the lower classes. It may be useful in higher classes.

(3) The time sense of the students should be developed by and by. In the beginning, the students should be acquainted with the events of the present and then an attempt should be made to take them back to the past.

(4) The law of cause and effect must be utilised in teaching at every stage of education.

(5) The teacher should invariably proceed from 'simple to complex' and 'concrete to abstract'. He should try to localise tbe subject-matter .with the help of maps and charts etc.

(6) An attempt should be made to co-relate the present experiences with the past.

(7) Dramatization and other activity methods make history interesting and real.

(8) The facts should be treated fully at the time of presentation.

(9) While teaching history, effect should be made to throw light on the various aspects of the history. Unnecessary and irrelevant materials should be discarded.

Presentation of Subject-matter of History at Primary Stage of Education

This stage of education runs up to fifth class where children between the age group of 6-11 years come for study. This is the stage when children are very fond of listening to stories. These stories may deal with any part of the world or any part of the life.

The teacher of history should try to present the subject-matter in the form of stories. These stories should encougage the activities of the children, The stories should also be told in an interesting manner.

In order to be a successful story-teller, the teacher should have perfect command over the subject-matter. He should also be well aware of the psychology of the students.

The stories should be so arranged that they may continue to awaken the curiosity of the students, to know things by saying and doing, and also get n with the historical materials.

Blackboard of Teacher should make a good deal of use of blackboard at parimary stage of education. He can safely, divide the subject-matter of history into various parts, and with the help of balckboard, present the subject-matter in the form of a story.

In the end, the teacher may put down the substance of the subject taught. After substance has been put down and written by the students, he can proceed on to the next part of the topic.

As already stated, the use of the blackboard should be made cautiously and discreetly. There should be a nice blackboard and the teacher should write on it legibly. Pictures, maps etc. may also be drawn on the blackboard with the help of coloured chalks.

Use of Pictures, Charts, Models, Maps etc. All these thing are visual aids. They catch the eyes of students and make the teaching interesting. The teacher should try to use these materials but in a cautious manner.

Pictures, charts, etc. should be accurate attractive and interesting. If models are presented before the students, they shall be able to have a correct-idea of the things which the models represent.

Too much use of these teaching aids, sometimes takes the students away from the real subject-matter of history, and that is why, these have to be used cautiously.

Text-books. In regard to the use of text-books at this stage of education, there is good deal of difference of opinion. Some educationists are of the view that text-books may be used discreetly, while others are of the opinion that text-books should not be used earlier than the class V.

It shall not be wrong to use text-books at this stage of education, but text-books should be written with an eye on the psychology of the students. They should be written in a simple language and in the mother tongue of the children.

The greatest advantage of the text-books is that the students can revise their lessons at home.

Time Sense. The time sense of the students, at this stage of education, should be developed. This can be done by arranging the stories in the chronological order of the time. The teacher should clearly indicate the relationship of the stories from the point of view of time. This can also be done with the help of charts, maps, etc.

Activity of the Students in the Teaching of History. Modern method of teaching lays a good deal of stress on the activity of students in the teaching of history. While teaching history to the students of the primary classes, the teacher should keep in mind that the students should also remain active. The teaching should be so arranged that the students take active part in the lesson. This can be done by bringing in the elements of drama dialogue or monologue in teaching.

Presentation of History at the Junior Stage of Education

This is the stage of education which arranges for teaching of classas VI, VII and VIII. Children of the age group of 11-14 years come here to receive education. This is the stage of education when the children are moving towards adolescence. Now, they do not take interest in listening to stories. By this time, children have become more realistic. Their memory, reasoning etc. have also developed by now. Therefore, the teaching of history at this stage of education should be organised on the psychological principles as enumerated below:

(1) Stress can be laid on the element of characterisation in the subject-matter.

(2) The facts should be properly explained before the studants. An attempt may be made to assess their value in the light of the problems of the present-day.

(3) Time sense should be developed further.

Method of Presentation. Now the teacher shoul not tell stories to the students. He should try to present facts and events of history in a systematic and chronological manner but in an interesting way. While doing so, he should keep in view the procedure of 'proceeding from concrete to abstract'. An attempt should be made to co-relate the events of history with the problems of the society as they exist today.

Test-books. At this stage of education, the teacher should make greater use of text-books, but these text-books should not be read like story books in the class. They should be used by the students at home for preparing their lessons, that they have read in the class. These text-books should be written with an eye on the psychology of the students of this age *i.e.*, learning by doing.

Written Work and Home Task. At this stage of education, the students should be given home task. But this home task should be in accordance with the circumstances and requirements of the students.

The students should also be asked to do written work. Students should be asked to write essays on various topics. They may also be asked to write essays on historical events and things.

Blackboard. Blackboard shall be used very often. The teacher should try to illustrate the subject-matter on the blackboard. The substance should be put down on the blackboard and the students should be asked to develop the outlines at home.

Charts, Maps, Models etc. Maps and charts should be used at this stage. The students should be helped to localise things and events with the help of maps.

These maps and charts should be properly drawn and based on the scientific data.

Map Drawing. Students at this stage of education, should be encouraged to draw maps. They may also be asked to fill in the places of historical importance in the maps. These things may also be given as home task.

Elements of Drama. At this stage of education, the students may be asked to dramatise and enact the various scenes of history. They may also be asked to speak out certain dialogues in the manner they have been presented to them.

Presentation of the History at the Secondary Stage of Education

This stage of education has classes IX, X, XI and XII where boys of 14 to 18 years of age come for education. This is the ago when the students have reached adolescence. The teaching should be so organised that it may meet the requirements of adolescence.

Self-activity and 'Learning by Doing'. Students at this stage of education are fond of doing things by themselves. They try to solve problems in a scientific manner of their own. Presentation of the subject-matter of history should be such that these psychological requirements of the students are met. Exhibits and pictures have an important role to play at this stage.

The teacher should try to present certain problems before the students and then he should encourage them to solve those problems. He should not interfere with the working of the students, but at the same time, keep a vigilant eye on the working, lest the students lose the focal point.

Blackboard. Blackboard should be used by the teacher. Substance may be written on it and the students should be asked to develop tbe substance. Sketches may be drawn on the blackboard and the subject-matter may be explained with the help these sketches.

Text-books. Text-books should be used freely at this stage at education. These text-books should be scientifically written. Students should be asked to prepare lesson at home with the help of these text-books.

Classroom Discussions. The teacher should arrange for classroom discussions on certain important topics and places of history. The students should be encouraged to take part in it, This method will be useful for developing the power of expression of students and doing away with their shyness. While the method is used, the teacher should be quite cautious. He should not allow irrelevant things to enter into the discussion.

Written Work. Students should be encouraged to do a good deal of written work at this stage of education. They should be given certain questions and asked to write out their answers at home. These answers should be corrected by the teacher and suggestions should be given to improve their working.

Source Method. At this stage of education, 'Source method' may be employed in the teaching of history. The students should be encouraged to study the original sources and with the help of those sources, the relevant matter may be collected. The students may be encouraged to do this job independently.

Organisations and Associations. At this stage of education, students should be asked to organise voluntary bodies in order to encourage the teaching of history. The members of such associations may be asked to divide themselves into groups. Each group should take to one task, such as collection of coins, old documents, and other rare things. At the meetings of these associations, the students should be asked to report about the work done by each group.

Familiarity with the Present-day Administration. The children should know something about the present-day administration. Only in that case they can be efficient citizens. As history is to be followed topically and the modern period is recommended for study, present-day administration will be t ιught through various topics. But the development of the present administration system should be taken up as a separate topic for intensive study also. The work should be made interesting and stimulating. There should be discussions also on such topics. Pupils should be encouraged to read newspapers.

Extra Reading. Pupils at this stage, should be encouraged to study extra books which may add to their knowledge of history. Source books if available, are really useful. During this stage, children should verify and supplement through sources what they have learnt from the text-books and the teacher.

Chronological and Concentric Presentation of History

History of India from ancient ages to modern times, is a very long course. In fact, the whole course cannot be taught in a year or even in a single stage. But all the Indian children are not fortunate enough to go beyond primary stage. Some of them complete middle stage and only few reach higher stage. The course of history is spread over many years. Two methods are followed while spreading the course over a long time. One is the concentric method, and the other the choronological method. In case of the former, efforts are made to finish the whole course in a single stage and to repeat it again and again in the next stage; the process being more detailed in the higher stages. In the chronological method, the course of history is divided into definite periods and each period is allotted to a particular class or stage. The process is detailed and uniform throughout. Generally, the history of India is divided into the following periods:

(1) Hindu period :

(a) Ancient Hindu period

(b) Historical Hindu period

(c) Rajput period.

(2) Muslim period:

(a) Sultanat.

(b) Moghuls.

(3) British period:

(a) The rule of the East India Company.

(b) India under the Crown.

MERITS OF COACENTRIC METHOD

The merits of this method are as follows :

(1) Young children cannot pursue history in detail. They cannot generalise and understand causal relations. Detailed study is not possible in early stages. Young children are more interested in stories than in scientific study of history. By and by, their scientific approach and the power of understanding and reasoning develops. Therefore, in every coming stage, the treatment happens to be more and more detailed.

(2) Most of our children have to leave school at the completion of the first stage. Through concentric method, even a child

of fifth class is aware of the outlines of the whole of Indian history.

(3) Knowledge of the subject in parts, is not desirable and meaningful. Children are very curious by nature. They wish to know the whole story of the the historical development. In this method, they are left in suspense.

DEMERITS OF THE CONCENTRIC METHOD

The demerits of this method are as follows:

(1) There is much repetitior. Generally, the pupils in the school of primary stage have to repeat the same history three times. It is nothing but loss of time. Moreover, it makes the subject dry and uninteresting.

(2) Pupils cannot develop time sense as the history of thousands of years is finished in a very short period.

(3) Really detailed study is never possible as the whole history is to be repeated in every new year or stage. Therefore, time is always short to give it a detailed treatment.

MERITS OF THE CHRONOLOGICAL METHOD

The merits of this method are as follows:

(1) It is a logical method. The beginning of history is started in an early stage and end comes at the end of the studies.

(2) The course of history is too long to be covered in a year or two. Chronological method provides scope for detailed treatment.

(3) This method satisfies the exponents of the cultural epoch theory to some extent. Children start with the study of the prehistoric men who lived in jungles and caves as hunters. They ultimately reach the modern civilization, passing through all the stages of evolution.

DEMERITS OF CHRONOLOGICAL METHOD

The demerits of this method are as follows:

(1) Young pupils cannot follow history in detail with full understanding. Therefore, the period which falls in the early stages, suffers permanently as it is never to be repeated.

(2) Some portions are too difficult but everything must be followed chronologically.

(3) Pupils are likely to forget the periods which they study in early stages.

(4) Generally, our children leave school without reaching the higher classes. Therefore, they are never able to go through the whole course of history.

(5) Children are curious by nature, but they have to remain in suspense for a long time due to the fact that they reach modern period of history after a long time.

Both the methods have their own merits and demerits. We should not be dependent upon anyone method exclusively. It is better to blend both the methods in such a way that students may get the benefit of both of them. At the primary stage, history should be presented purely in the form of social studies blended and integrated with geography civics and sociology. The same treatment should be followed in the middle stage, but history should get more importance as a distinct subject also. Purely chronologieal treatment should be followed in higher classes.

❑